On the Road *with the*
Legendary Heroes *of* Hockey

GREY*S*TONE BOOKS
Douglas & McIntyre Publishing Group
Vancouver/Toronto/Berkeley

Greystone Books
A division of Douglas & McIntyre Ltd.
2323 Quebec Street, Suite 201
Vancouver, British Columbia
Canada v5T 4S7
www.greystonebooks.com

National Library of Canada Cataloguing in Publication Data
Mason, Gary
   Oldtimers

   Includes index.
   ISBN 1-55054-939-1 (bound) 1-55054-890-5 (paper)

   1. Hockey players—Canada—Biography. 2. Hockey players—
United States—Biography. 3. National Hockey League—Anecdotes. I. Title.
GV848.5.A1M37 2002   796.962′092′2   C2002-911007-6

Library of Congress Cataloging-in-Publication data is available.

"Honky, the Christmas Goose," quoted on page 41, was recorded by Johnny Bower
and Little John with the Rinky Dinks and was released by Capitol Records (72318)
in 1965.

Editing by John Eerkes-Medrano
Cover design by Peter Cocking and Jessica Sullivan
Text design by Peter Cocking
Cover photograph of Tiger Williams (left) and Paul Reinhart (right)
by North Light Images/Stuart McCall
Typesetting by Rhonda Ganz
Printed and bound in Canada by Friesens
Printed on acid-free paper ∞
Distributed in the U.S. by Publishers Group West

We gratefully acknowledge the financial support of the Canada Council for the
Arts, the British Columbia Arts Council, and the Government of Canada through
the Book Publishing Industry Development Program (BPIDP) for our publishing
activities.

CONTENTS

To my mother, whom I loved deeply and miss terribly,

and my father, who remains my greatest hero.

PREFACE

My two favourite memories as a boy both involve hockey. Growing up in Chippawa, Ontario, I can vividly recall my first years in minor hockey and being woken by my mother at five o'clock in the morning for a weekend practice or game. My father, a shift worker at the local plant, always seemed to be either at work or in bed getting some sleep before heading to work, so the job of taking me to the rink generally fell to my mom. I can still hear her scraping the frost off the windshield of the car and starting it up so that it would be warm when I jumped inside. I remember always going for French fries after my games. The first hockey sweater Santa ever brought me was blue and white and had a maple leaf on it. But when I got a little older it was the Detroit Red Wings I loved.

Which brings me to my second memory, which, I'm aware, is one every other kid growing up in Canada in the 1960s also had: watching *Hockey Night in Canada* on Saturday nights. I remember being stretched out in front of the only television set we had in the house, on my stomach, always in my hockey pajamas. My favourite snack was cream soda pop and potato chips. Gordie Howe and Johnny Bower and Ted Lindsay were my heroes, as were Bobby Hull and Stan Mikita and Davie Keon. As I got older they were replaced by Bobby Orr, my favourite hockey player of all time, and Phil Esposito and Derek Sanderson. I loved Turk Sanderson and bragged to friends that he once dated my oldest sister. Later, when my family moved to Sarnia, Ontario, hockey was as big a part of my life as ever. Sarnia was, and remains, one of the great hockey towns in Canada, and when I was growing up there it was a factory for producing NHL players. Tony McKegney, who played 912 games in the NHL for eight different teams, grew up right behind our house. Mike Crombeen, who played minor hockey with Tony, later played 475 games in the NHL, mostly for the St. Louis Blues. He grew up three blocks behind me. Wayne Merrick, who won four Stanley Cups with the New York Islanders, took over my Sarnia *Observer* paper route when we were kids and used it to train. Whereas most carriers would pack their papers on the front of their bikes, I remember Wayne running around the streets of our neighbourhood with his bag slung over his shoulder. Dino Ciccarelli, who played more than 1,200 games in the NHL, grew up on Mitton Street, two blocks west of where I lived.

This is all to say that I have had more than an abiding interest in hockey and the NHL as long as I can remember. Getting an opportunity to travel and play alongside some of the hockey greats I watched as a young boy and later as a teenager and university student was more than a great assignment. It was a dream come true. Books are always a collaborative effort, and when they are completed there is generally a long list of people to be thanked. This book is no exception. So here goes. To anyone I have forgotten—and I'm sure there will be a few—I apologize now. Please know that I appreciated your assistance, small or large. This book would not have been done without the cooperation of the fine people at Xentel DM, which runs the Oldtimers tour. Special thanks go to Cathy Sproule, an amazing and tireless worker who always had time for my questions, and Avi Sarkar, who made sure I was taken care of at all of our stops. I want to thank Tiger Williams, who encouraged me every step of the way and gave me some of the best insights into the game I could have found anywhere. I appreciated the beers we shared and look forward to a few more in the future. To Gary Nylund, Paul Reinhart, Mark Napier and Jimmy Mann, thank you all for the extra time you gave me and the friendship that always went along with it. I want to thank all the Oldtimers for sharing their thoughts and ice time with me and above all for making me feel a welcome member of their very exclusive club. I am lucky to work at a place like the *Vancouver Sun*. I am lucky to have a publisher like Dennis Skulsky and an editor like Neil Reynolds. I am lucky to have friends like executive editor Shelley Fralic and managing editor Patricia Graham, whose support over the years has meant so much to me. To my sports editor, Steve Snelgrove, thanks for being so understanding about my taking time off. Of course, this project would never been done without a publisher, and I was fortunate enough to land one of the best. I'd like to thank Rob Sanders at Greystone Books for first believing in this idea and then believing in me as a writer. I'd like to thank Nancy Flight, as fine a person as she is an editor. To John Eerkes-Medrano, who evened out all the bumps in my copy and made me look better than I deserve, thank you, sir, for your brilliant handiwork. Thanks to Peter Cocking for the great cover and Kelly Mitchell for all her efforts to promote this book. Finally, my greatest source of inspiration, as always, comes from my family. To my wonderful wife, Barbara, and my two awesome boys, Jordan and Geoffrey, all I can say is I'm the luckiest guy alive.

PROLOGUE

THE BAR SEEMED to be empty that afternoon. It was only when I stepped around the corner that I saw Tiger Williams sitting at a table with someone I didn't immediately recognize in the dim light.

As I got closer, I could see that the mystery guest was Doug Gilmour of the Montreal Canadiens, who was in Vancouver with his team to play the Canucks the following night. The Lions Pub was conveniently located behind the Waterfront Hotel, a five-star establishment that overlooked Coal Harbour and had become a popular choice among visiting NHL teams, including the Canadiens. The Lions, as it was known to those who frequented it, had become a busy lunch and after-work destination for the downtown office crowd that enjoyed the bar's comfortable surroundings as well as the menu's long list of lagers, stouts and ales. Gilmour had popped over for a pint himself when he saw Williams, and the two began exchanging stories.

Gilmour was thirty-eight but looked younger, which was surprising for someone who had eaten as many fists, elbows, butt ends. Sure there were a few scars here and there, but there wasn't a speck of grey on his head. Years of late nights and early wake-up calls and beers with the boys hadn't appeared to take any toll on him. Not externally anyway. It was apparent Gilmour was in his element here, sharing beers and stories with an old friend, finding out what had become of old teammates.

Also apparent was that Gilmour was "old school" all the way and yearned for the days when he shared the ice with guys like Williams, players who loved hockey and strove to be the best but also knew how to have a good time. In some ways, Gilmour didn't even recognize the young players coming into the league today.

The Canadiens had recently called up an eighteen-year-old goaltender, Olivier Michaud, because of injuries to their regular netminders. Suddenly, Gilmour found himself looking across the dressing room at a teammate who wasn't even born when he was drafted in 1982. Michaud, in fact, was born on September 14, 1983, when Gilmour was stepping onto the ice for his first training camp with the St. Louis Blues.

If Gilmour needed any more reminders of how old he was getting, he only had to look at Habs linemate Chad Kilger. Kilger's dad, Bob, had coached Gilmour in the Ontario Hockey League with the 1981 Memorial Cup champion Cornwall Royals. Chad was four at the time.

Besides being younger than he was, today's players were different, too, Gilmour was saying. Instead of popping aspirin to relieve a hangover from the night before, today's players went to bed right after the game and popped high-octane vitamins to give them a competitive edge. "I don't know, Tiger," Gilmour said, wrapping his hand around another pint. "Some of the fun has definitely been lost. The guys coming in now are really different."

As an example, Gilmour cited a recent stopover by the Canadiens in Edmonton. As the team was piling off the bus for a practice, Gilmour asked a young teammate who was injured and wasn't practising if he would mind getting twenty-four beers for the boys to enjoy later. When practice finished, Gilmour showered and headed to the back of the bus, ready to enjoy a few cold ones with some of his like-minded teammates. "Where's the beer?" Gilmour asked the rookie, as he settled into his seat. His young teammate looked sheepish and then slowly pulled out a six-pack of Molson Canadian from his coat pocket. "That's it?" Gilmour asked. "A six-pack is all you got?" The player didn't know what to say. "Next time I'll get it myself," Gilmour sighed.

Yes, players were different today; perhaps some of that had to do with the incredible sums of money that could now be made in an NHL uniform. It was worth the sacrifice of eschewing beer, forcing a few vitamins down your throat, working out harder than a triathlete, because a few good years could set a player up for life. No one knew that better than Gilmour. But while the dedication of today's hockey player was understandable, there was something lamentable about it too.

"There's not nearly as many good stories," said Gilmour.

Listening to the two hockey players share their tales from the trenches that afternoon gave you the sense that not only was some of the fun gone from the game but also some of the loyalty and camaraderie that once existed among players. Hockey was all business now. Someone who was a teammate today could be the enemy tomorrow. No one stayed in one place for long anymore.

The best stories Gilmour had were not from the last few years of his career, with the Buffalo Sabres and now with the Canadiens. His favourite memories were from much earlier, when he was breaking into the NHL as a bug-eyed rookie, fresh out of junior. Gilmour remembered his first training camp with the Blues and laying in bed late one night waiting for his roommate, Brian Sutter, to return to the hotel after a night out with the boys.

"I can't remember exactly when he stumbled in, but it was late and the room was pitch dark, and I had my little duffel bag with everything I owned at the bottom of my bed," Gilmour recalled. "Anyway, Brian came in and tripped over my bag and ended up crashing into the window in the room.

"He started screaming at me and I just pulled my blanket up over my head and pretended to be asleep. But I was scared. All those Sutters were tough. Man, were they tough."

Gilmour talked about his days with the Leafs and the Western Conference finals in 1994 against the Canucks.

"I remember that series against the Canucks was tough," Gilmour said smiling. "Gino (Odjick) was on my case one game. Just giving it to me every chance he got. Giving me the stick, you name it. So Wendel (Clark) lines up with Pavel (Bure) for a faceoff. He says, 'You'd better tell your buddy Odjick to lay off of Gilmour or I'll fix you so you won't finish this game. Understand?'"

Bure didn't say a thing, but the message was apparently communicated. Odjick didn't bother Gilmour the rest of the series.

And so it went that afternoon. One story from Gilmour was matched by another from Tiger. Outside, the afternoon light faded and was replaced by a chilly darkness. As the hours passed by, Gilmour was phoned by teammates asking if he wanted to join them for dinner.

"I'm just here having a bowl of soup with Tiger Williams," Gilmour said, smiling as another round arrived.

It was clear Gilmour didn't want to leave the company of a former NHLer he could relate to so well. Someone who was "old school," just like him. You realized as you sat there listening to them talk that this visit could last for many more hours, days probably, before they were finished swapping stories. That is what you did in the NHL, it occurred to me. You collected paycheques, yes, but you also collected stories and memories, things that were far more valuable.

As pleased as Gilmour was to be playing another year and

making $2 million US for doing it, you got the feeling he'd easily trade it for the first years of his career again and his time as a Leaf captain, when there were still characters in the game and the NHL was a travelling circus that rolled into town, set up shop for a night and then left under the cover of darkness along with so many tales.

But as much as Gilmour seemed to long for the old days, you also got the feeling that if he could he would play hockey until he was eighty—even if it was in some rec league. That was how much he loved the game, how intoxicating he found the odour of a dressing room.

Williams told Gilmour about the Oldtimers Hockey Challenge, of which he had become part. He rhymed off the names of some of the players who often played, guys who loved a beer now and then, guys who were "old school"—just like "Killer" Gilmour himself.

"You'll have to play with us when you finally retire," Williams said to Gilmour as the pair took final tugs on their beers.

"You know," said Gilmour, "I'd love to. I feel like an Oldtimer anyway."

CHAPTER I

HERE'S JOHNNY!

"Has anyone seen Johnny?"

Our flight for Whitehorse was due to leave in half an hour. Everyone on the team had arrived and exchanged handshakes and asked about families. But the coach was still nowhere to be found. And we weren't going anywhere without Johnny Bower.

For over an hour the scene in the boarding lounge had resembled a reunion—in this case, an NHL reunion. Russ Courtnall was talking with his long-ago teammate from the Toronto Maple Leafs, Gary Nylund. Doug Bodger was chatting with Bob Rouse about players they knew in a common stopover with the San Jose Sharks. Marcel Dionne was laughing about something Jimmy Mann, the former tough guy with the Winnipeg Jets, had just told him. Paul Reinhart, the smooth-skating defenceman with the Calgary Flames and Vancouver Canucks, was enjoying a conversation with Wayne Babych, whose best NHL years were with the St. Louis Blues.

We had defencemen, we had forwards, we had a goaltender, but still no coach.

"We're going to have to fine him," someone said.

"Fine him?" said Tiger Williams. "I'm going to plough the prick as soon as I see him."

The team was coming together already.

It was called the Oldtimers Hockey Challenge. Which was really just a fancy name for the tour that took place across Canada every year involving former NHL hockey players. What had started nearly twenty-five years earlier as a few games involving mostly French-speaking former NHLers from the Montreal Canadiens, the Oldtimers tour was now a big-budget, cross-continental affair managed by Xentel DM, a large marketing firm headquartered in Calgary.

For the 2001–02 season, Xentel had rolled out an ambitious forty-four-game, four-tour campaign. The first tour, the one we were leaving on, opened in the far north before moving into British Columbia and Alberta. The second tour would begin in January in Montreal, before playing centres in the Maritimes and Ontario. The third series was almost exclusively played in Ontario, while the fourth and final one, which always included the biggest names, started in mid-March in Red Deer and finished at the Air Canada Centre in Toronto at the end of the month.

The makeup of the teams changed from tour to tour and in some cases before a tour had even ended, like on this one, which would see the team play an exhausting nineteen games in twenty-one nights. Even the circus wasn't that gruelling. In all, nearly thirty different NHLers would play in at least one of the games.

Because of his flamboyant nature and ability to entertain a crowd, Tiger Williams had been one of the first non–French-speaking players to be invited to play for the Oldtimers. Over the years, as the tour expanded, other English-speaking players were added. Players like Brad Park, the Hockey Hall of Fame defenceman, and Terry O'Reilly, the legendary Boston Bruins tough guy, were added to the team. Bobby Hull had also become a fixture on the tours, usually as a guest coach who spent most of his time signing autographs. Others who suited up included Guy Lafleur, Henri Richard, Mario Faubert, Jim Dorey, Mario Marois, Stan Mikita, Eddie Shack, Rick Smith and Norm Ullman.

But it had bothered Williams that when the Oldtimers played in western Canada there were few players in the lineup who had ever played for an NHL team in that part of the world. Because of the origins of the tour, most of the players continued to be French-speaking ex–Montreal Canadiens. Williams didn't have anything against the French, he just felt it was time to add some local flavour to the lineup, even if the players weren't big-name stars.

Williams argued that a born-and-bred western Canadian who made it to the big leagues would be appreciated in arenas in B.C. and Alberta and Saskatchewan and Manitoba more than an Yvon Lambert or Gaston Gingras or Richard Sevigny, Oldtimer regulars who were far bigger names in Quebec. Not that there was anything wrong with those guys, as Jerry Seinfeld might say. They just didn't have a local connection that might draw more people to the games. With the first tour of the 2001–02 Oldtimers campaign being played mostly in B.C. and Alberta, Williams thought this was the perfect opportunity to add some some familiar faces to the lineup.

All he had to do was convince the tour organizers.

This wasn't hard for Williams to do. He could be extremely persuasive, especially with a stick in his hand. Luckily, he didn't have to use one to convince Xentel to let him pick the players for the first tour, which would begin in Whitehorse and end in Lloydminster, Alberta, three weeks later. And so, after a couple of months of cajoling and arm-twisting, Williams had his lineup. Most of the players would only play a six-game block of the nineteen-game schedule. For the tour's first leg, which would begin in

Whitehorse, then move in order to Yellowknife, Inuvik and the Alaskan cities and towns of Fairbanks, Kenai and Anchorage, Williams had managed to assemble a pretty good group.

Every great team was built from the goal out, and the Old-timers had managed to snag one-time netminder extraordinaire—Richard Brodeur—to keep the pucks out during the northern swing. "King Richard," as he became known to Vancouver Canucks fans, would be forever remembered for his incredible streak of goaltending in 1982, when he helped lead the Canucks to the Stanley Cup finals against the New York Islanders. At fifty-one, Brodeur still had a wicked glove hand.

Then there was the defence, which was big, rangy and not without some speed and toughness. The blueline corps included Gary Nylund, a former first-rounder who saw his career end after eleven seasons due to a series of injuries. After being drafted by the Leafs and playing four seasons in Toronto, Nylund went on to play with the Chicago Blackhawks and New York Islanders. Now a thirty-nine-year-old firefighter near his home in White Rock, B.C., Nylund had the physique of someone twenty years younger and looked like he could still play in the big leagues.

Bob Rouse would also be on the blueline. Rouse had capped a seventeen-year NHL career with two Stanley Cup wins with the Detroit Red Wings in the late 1990s. Never flashy, Rouse was your standard issue stay-at-home, stick-in-your-ribs, glove-in-your-face defenceman who was built like a middle linebacker. Just a year removed from his playing days, he still had it all.

Rouse would often be paired during the trip with Doug Bodger. Like Rouse, Bodger had only recently hung up his skates, finishing his career with the Canucks after thirteen games in the 1999–2000 season. Little did any of us realize the stage presence Bodger would have during the trip.

And then there was Paul Reinhart. Was there anyone smoother on the Calgary Flames blueline during the 1980s? Or a defence-man more impressive on the Canucks blueline after his trade to

Vancouver in 1988? As intelligent a player as Reinhart was during his NHL days, we would learn that he saved his smartest moves until after he retired.

The forwards, meanwhile, would be led by Marcel Dionne. Although he didn't have the same set of wheels that he used to fly around on, the Hockey Hall of Famer could still make players half his age look awfully silly. There would be few arenas where he wouldn't get the loudest ovation of the evening.

Sometimes lining up alongside Dionne would be Russ Courtnall. Every Oldtimers tour needed a ringer, and Courtnall was ours. Not only did he look as young as the day he was drafted, he didn't appear to have lost a step on the ice either. It seemed absurd, saying Russ Courtnall and Oldtimer in the same breath.

It had been many years and many pounds since Wayne Babych scored fifty-four goals as a St. Louis Blue, but he was an all-round nice guy who seemed assured a spot on the Oldtimers tour as long as he wanted one. He would be joined up front by Mark Lofthouse.

A star in junior with the old New Westminster Bruins, Lofthouse never had the starry NHL career many predicted he would, but he could still skate and had a shot that could decapitate a moose.

Then there was Jimmy Mann. Most NHL tough guys could score goals before they got to The Show, and Mann was no exception. He, too, had been slowed down over the years by one too many burgers, but he could still put the puck in the net with amazing consistency. And, of course, you never knew when things might get out of hand.

Tiger, of course, would also be playing. While sometimes he could look like he'd seen the bottom of one too many beer bottles at five o'clock in the morning, nothing was ever as it appeared with Tiger. He was as sharp as a skate blade and had developed a shot that was harder than the one he had during his playing days.

And finally there was me.

While I was tagging along to chronicle life on the Oldtimers tour I was also there to play, when needed. I had suited up with the Oldtimers months earlier for my regular sports column in the *Vancouver Sun*. I played two games and had been encouraged by the comments of friends and colleagues.

"Well, you didn't make a complete fool out of yourself," one observed.

"Actually, you weren't as horrible as I expected," another added.

Which to me screamed: "I can play with these guys!"

During my first stint with the team, my Oldtimers teammates had tried desperately to get me a goal. As my last shifts with the team began to vanish, Brad Park urged me to stand in front of the net. "I'll try and bank a slapshot in off your ass," he said. "At this point I think it's the best we can hope for." No luck. My new teammates, however, emboldened by the supreme self-confidence and determination that helped get them to the NHL in the first place, assured me I would have a goal before our swing through the north was over.

"Don't get his hopes up," Williams told the players as we waited to board the plane. "You haven't seen him play yet."

Of course, it was all in the name of research. Playing with former NHL hockey players, even ones well past their prime, gave you a pretty good sense of just how skilled these guys were in their playing days. Initially, my biggest worry about playing with the Oldtimers was speed. Would I be so slow that I would look like an obvious impostor? Would I lag so far behind the play that I looked like a defenceman instead of the forward I was supposed to be?

As it turned out, it wasn't speed or keeping up that proved the biggest challenge. It was was handling their passes.

When you're sitting in your living room watching the NHL on TV or in a press box high above the action, you can't appreciate how fast the game truly is or how quickly players have to move the puck in order to survive. In most cases, moving the puck quickly means moving it hard. The first time a pass from Brad Park hit my stick, I had no better chance of corralling it than a six-year-old did. That's how unprepared I was for its sheer force.

But it wasn't really the puck I was after on this trip anyway. It was the stories.

Ask any retired hockey player what he misses most about the game and he won't say the money, the adulation, the best seats in the fanciest restaurants. He'll say it's the dressing room. It's sitting around in his hockey underwear before games and after practices, talking about old teams and old teammates, about the night this guy broke curfew in Toronto and the time that guy challenged the coach to a fight when he was drunk.

It was the Oldtimers' stories, as much as anything, that also best illustrated how much the game has changed over the years. The last of the old breed, guys like Doug Gilmour, who began his NHL career only a year after Bobby Hull officially ended his, were dying out. They had been replaced by athletes who were making more in a single year than some of the Oldtimers had made in a lifetime. The player today trained year-round, forever wary that one slip-up could mean losing his spot on the team to some hungry young turk pawing at the dressing room door.

Yes, today's NHL players could earn enough in a few years to set them up for life, but would their days as big-time hockey players be as good in the telling? Would the Paul Kariyas and Joe Sakics have nearly the stories to one day relate to others as players who toiled in the league years earlier did? Did it even matter to them? Or had professional sports become so serious, the scrutiny from the media so stifling, that a hockey player today couldn't carry on like his predecessors even if he wanted to?

There was another thing I was searching for too. The answer to why people still cared about these guys. How was it, I needed to know, that Marcel Dionne and Guy Lafleur and Frank Mahovlich and Yvan Cournoyer and Lanny McDonald and Darryl Sittler could sell out the Skyreach Centre in Edmonton or the Saddledome in Calgary? Did they really have that kind of impact on people when they played? Did hockey fans today love yesterday's heroes more than they admired Eric Lindros or Mats Sundin? Did people remember the guys who played the game years ago being more approachable than they are today?

Maybe fans who came out to see us play sensed this was the last group of former NHL players who would play to one-thousand-seat arenas around Canada and Alaska for no better reason than wanting to give something back to the game. Maybe that's what this was all about—saying thanks.

Back in the boarding lounge, Doug Bodger was sitting with his elbows resting on his knees. Bob Rouse and Mark Lofthouse and a few others were sitting in chairs around him, listening. It was story time already.

Bodger was telling the boys about the time in New Jersey when Jacques Lemaire, then coaching the Devils, confronted the players in practice over some beer found on the team bus. At the time, the Devils were a powerhouse, sailing along in first place, a pleasant change for Bodger, who had recently come to the team from the then-lowly San Jose Sharks.

Bodger dusted off his worst French accent to imitate Lemaire.

"I sink dares been some drinking on de bus," Bodger recalled Lemaire saying to the assembled players. "I want to know what goes on."

Lemaire looked around waiting for someone to say something. There wasn't a word. He surveyed the players looking for the most most obvious culprits. He found Doug Gilmour.

"Doug, what do you know?"

Gilmour played it down: "It's nothing serious, Jacques. A couple of beers. It's not a big deal."

Not satisfied, Lemaire went to another player who gave the coach much the same answer. A few beers. Not a big deal. Don't sweat it.

Still not satisfied, Lemaire looked at his newest player, Doug Bodger, a happy-go-lucky type known to enjoy the odd lager.

"Doug, what do you know?"

Leaning on his hockey stick, Bodger looked at his coach.

"Jacques," Bodger said. "All I know is, if it ain't broke don't fix it. We're in first place. Who cares if we're drinking?"

Everyone laughed. Bodger, it was easy to tell, was the kind of person coaches and teammates liked to call a "good guy to have in the room." Which meant he was a player's player, enjoyed by his teammates as much for his good nature off the ice as for the skills he possessed on it.

"They got more than a foot of snow in Whitehorse last night," someone said.

There were a few groans, but as we looked outside the weather in Vancouver was typically dreary for November. The rain was constant. There is no sky to speak of, only a dull, gun-metal-grey canopy of clouds that made you feel like you were sitting inside of a domed stadium.

"Johnny!" someone yelled.

All eyes turned as our coach walked slowly towards us.

Johnny Bower was smiling. He was wearing a leather Maple Leafs jacket and brown corduroys. There was a slight hobble to his step. Soon he was amid the players and there were lots of hugs and handshakes. A legend was in the room, and everyone seemed to know it.

I had grown up with Johnny Bower. He was on the television in our living room, on my bedroom walls, on my hockey cards. My mind has lost many things over the years, but my memory of those Saturday nights in front of the television watching the Toronto Maple Leafs are strangely vivid. I can remember exactly where the couch was that my parents used to sit on to watch the game and where the TV was in relation to it. I remember my parents used to watch *Don Messer's Jubilee* afterwards.

And I remember Johnny Bower, the greatest goalie in the world.

Of all the players from that era, Bower and Gordie Howe were the two who fascinated me most. I'm not even sure why. But they did. I wasn't even a big Leafs fan. I cried when the Buds beat the Wings for the Cup in 1964. But I thought Johnny Bower was something else. Maybe it was because he had toiled for so many years in the minors before he got his break. But I doubt I even knew that when I was eight and nine and ten years old. Maybe it was just his face. It seemed old for a hockey player, but it also seemed kind. As strange as it sounds, that's how I always thought of Johnny Bower—as a wonderfully kind and humble man.

And now here he was, in the flesh, looking, well, exactly like I remember Johnny Bower looking. Maybe with a few more wrinkles and maybe with ears that seemed too big for his head. But his smile was just how I remembered it. How could you forget that smile?

"I guess we can leave now that the coach has goddamn well finally decided to show up," said Tiger, trying to keep a straight face.

"You weren't getting worried, were you?" Johnny laughed.

It was time to go.

The players began grabbing their carry-on bags. We were heading to the land of the Midnight Sun where there would only be a few hours of light a day. The players appeared as excited as children on the first day of school.

"We're starting to jell," Wayne Babych said to me. "I can feel it. Can you feel it? Come on, tell me you feel it."

CHAPTER 2

THE SNIPE HUNT

Several of the players strained their necks to get a peek out the window as we began our descent into the Yukon capital of Whitehorse, but there was little to see. The weather report we had received hours earlier was correct. It had snowed, seemingly for days.

The Yukon River, which runs through downtown Whitehorse, gurgled under a fresh blanket of the white stuff. Lake Schwatka, which long ago had flooded the famous rapids that inspired the city's name, slept under a coat of it too. The ss *Klondike,* which once plied the Yukon's wondrous river system, sat docked at the end of Second Avenue, frozen in time.

It was dark and unpleasant-looking outside, with heavy grey clouds squatting above the city. It was the kind of day you imagined might have compelled prospectors here eighty years earlier to go watch Snake-Hips Lulu and Mollie Fewclothes at the local dance hall instead of mining for gold.

"Is this where you get the sour-toe cocktails?" someone near the back of the plane yelled out.

"That's Dawson," came the reply.

"What about ice worms?"

"Don't think so."

"Then what the hell are we doing here?"

The plane touched down quietly. We had been told that the Whitehorse airport had the world's largest weather vane. And sure enough, there it was, a restored 1942 DC-3 that moved so it always faced the wind. Local members of the RCMP were waiting with vans to take us to our hotel, the High Country Inn. We were there in minutes, and were greeted by a two-storey-high model of a Mountie. Looking at this giant, you could imagine the marketing possibilities: "Come stay at the The High Country Inn— Home of the World's Largest Wooden Mountie!!!!"

I hopped into a small elevator on the main floor with Gary Nylund. A middle-aged woman and another man were cramped in it with us. The woman sized Nylund up, from his toes to his eyebrows, and deduced by his jacket he was with some kind of hockey team.

"Who do you play for?" she asked.

Just then the elevator door opened to Nylund's floor.

"We're called the Oldtimers," he said as he backed out. "Also known as the Has-beens."

The door closed. The woman looked at me.

"He doesn't look like an oldtimer to me. Wow."

Game time was seven o'clock, four hours away. Long enough for some guys to grab naps if they wanted or to get some lunch. I wasn't playing, deciding it would be better to spend the first game of the tour soaking up the atmosphere. I ended up going over to the Takhini Arena about an hour before game time. Since it had been built in the mid-eighties, the Takhini had become a focal point for local entertainment. "We've had monster trucks and those famous Lipizzaner stallions in there," said the woman at the hotel's front desk. And now the Oldtimers.

It wasn't the first time the tour had come to town. Years earlier—Tiger Williams couldn't remember the precise year—the Oldtimers caused a near-riot when organizers sold more tickets than there was space. People started banging and kicking the doors before the police arrived to quell the growing dissent. On this night there seemed to be a smooth flow of spectators into the arena. People arrived in snowmobile suits and heavy parkas. Some wore their favourite hockey jersey over their winter coats. The smell of french fries and nachos wafted through the lobby.

Brenda Williams, Tiger's wife and the only spouse travelling on the tour, set up a souvenir table in the main lobby. There was an odd assortment of items, ranging from the predictable— miniature autographed hockey sticks ($10), miniature autographed goalie sticks ($25), rugby shirts ($35), hockey pencils ($2)—to things like Tiger's long-since-published autobiography and a souvenir plate with Tiger's image on it, in which he was wearing jerseys of three of the NHL teams he played for. The prices of these items appeared to be negotiable.

In the dressing room the players got ready.

Jimmy Mann was telling the boys about an Oldtimers game years ago in Victoria. Gary "Suitcase" Smith, whose NHL career had taken him to so many cities, including Toronto, Oakland, Chicago and Vancouver, was the team's goalie.

"A few hours before the game he tells us he's not going to play," Mann told the guys. "He's come up with some story about the boyfriend of an old girlfriend having threatened to shoot him if he played in the game. Shoot him right at the rink. Smith believed him and said he wasn't going to play. Anyway, the local organizer gets wind of it and says he's not going to pay us unless Smith plays in the game. So now we're sweating.

"Anyway, we finally reach Smith at the hotel where we were

staying. He's just getting ready to check out. Someone gets him on the phone and says, 'Listen, you son of a bitch. Unless you play tonight we're not getting paid, so you'd better get your ass down here and play.'"

Money triumphed over sense; Smith eventually did show up, and he lived to tell about it.

"Smitty was a beauty," Mann continued. "I played with him in Winnipeg. It was near the end of his career. One night we went into Philly. Smith was the backup. We skated on the ice for the pre-game skate, and the fans are booing us and screaming and Smith is raising his arms in the air in triumph, egging the fans on. We're all looking at him like he's nuts. 'Why are you doing this, Smitty?' Anyway, the game gets going and we get a three-goal lead. We're thinking we might just win this thing.

"Then our goalie gets hurt. I can't remember who it was. But he gets hurt and we have to put Smith in. Well, you can imagine what the fans were like when they see him, eh? They just go crazy. They're screaming at him, just really giving it to him. Well, I think the first four shots or something against him go in, and we lose the game. The coach was furious. It was the last game Gary Smith ever played as a Jet."

The game against a team of local RCMP officers and firemen was now ten minutes away. Ron Hoggarth, the former NHL referee, walked to the centre of the dressing room and asked for the players' attention. Hoggarth was on the tour as sort of an on-ice master of ceremonies. His job: to crack jokes, make sure the crowd didn't fall asleep and help with prearranged gags. He began handing each player a red ball.

"When you throw these balls on the ice they start to glow," said Hoggarth, beginning to explain the gag. "So when you go out to get introduced, hide the ball in your glove. Then after the intros, while the arena is still dark, someone will go first and throw the ball on the ice and then everyone falls in behind him. What I want you to do is skate around in a figure eight or something with the balls—it will look really cool—and then I'll be checking the net out and then you come in and fire the balls at me. Got it?"

There was silence.

"I don't know, Hoggie," Marcel Dionne finally said. "I don't know if it's going to work all that well."

"Oh, it will work, trust me," Hoggarth said. "It'll be great."

Around the room, the players exchanged bewildered looks.

"Ohhhh-kay, we'll try the lighted red ball trick," Nylund deadpanned, cracking everyone up.

The red balls were made of a hard plastic and were hard to control on the ice. The players had no idea what the balls were going to do when they began shooting them at Hoggarth for the first time. One of the first shots taken was by Wayne Babych. The ball, which must have been travelling 80 mph, missed Hoggarth's head by inches. Had it hit him it likely would have knocked him out cold. But instead of mothballing the gag, Hoggarth insisted on using it throughout the tour. There would be many more close calls.

THE BEGINNING of each Oldtimers game was the same. The players were introduced to a thumping disco beat while strobe lights flashed around the arena. After the last player was introduced, the announcer said: "Ladies and gentleman, your legendary hockey heroes." At which point mini-fireworks were set off and the crowd worked itself into a frenzy.

In theory, at least.

On this tour, Xentel decided to tie in the events of September 11 with the on-ice proceedings. Almost every team the Oldtimers would play had representatives from the local RCMP or fire department. Usually, the team presented the NHLers with a hat or T-shirt before the game that was emblazoned with the name and hall number of their department. Before the national anthems were sung, the crowd was treated to Celine Dion's rendition of "God Bless America" while kids from the local figure skating association skated around the ice carrying U.S. and Canadian flags.

As hokey as it sounded, it worked. At least in the small towns. A teenaged girl sang both national anthems in English, and she then sang a French version of the Canadian anthem from a song-sheet. Her hands were trembling, and when it was over the crowd gave her a warm ovation for her courage.

"Whitehorse, are you ready for some fun tonight?" said Hoggarth, sounding like the lead singer of a band. "I can't hear you! Are you ready for some fun tonight?"

Hoggarth then set off, looking for a few local saps to work into his routine.

"Look at this guy in the Boston Bruins jersey," he boomed into his cordless mike as he pointed to some guy in the first row.

"Loser."

Then he was off to find someone else.

"Where'd you get that haircut, buddy? Canadian Tire?"

The crowd loved it and was having more fun than the team of RCMP officers and firemen who would become the Oldtimers' first victims on the tour. Were it not for a goalie who decided to impersonate Dominik Hasek, the score would have been 15–0 after the first period. With five minutes still left in the opening frame, the Oldtimers had already rifled thirty shots in the poor guy's direction but had only four goals to show for it.

The opposition wasn't great, but it wasn't brutal either. There were some players who could skate. And some players who could shoot. But as a team, the cops and firefighters were no match for Nylund and Courtnall, Marcel and Tiger.

The NHLers would score twice more before the end of the first period and head to the dressing room with a 6–0 lead.

By the time I wandered down, Tiger was already in mid-story, this one about Guy Lafleur and the time he let a slapshot go from just inside the faceoff circle in this very same rink.

"Well, the puck hits the goalie right in the mask, eh," Williams was saying, laughing at the memory. "And he's wearing one of those wire-mesh cages. Well, the shot bent the wire caging right in, and the guy's nose is bleeding like crazy. Well, the crazy pricks on his team start trying to yank the guy's mask off and they're pulling and pulling and the guy is just screaming, "Ahhhh, ahhhh, it's caught, it's caught!

"Well, what happened was the wire bent in so much it was caught under the guy's nose. They're trying to pull the helmet off and they're almost ripping the poor guy's nose off because the wire's right underneath it. It was a mess. It was right after that we decided to ban slapshots in these games."

Just as Williams finished his tale, dozens of lucky program holders began pouring into the dressing room to get autographs and pictures taken with their hockey heroes. They were mostly children, some of whom were with parents who wanted to say hi and thanks to players they had watched as kids themselves.

Tiger's stall, it was quickly apparent, would become a favourite stop among the autograph hunters.

"Daddy used to watch this man play hockey at Pacific Coliseum," one man said to his son as Williams signed his program.

Then a little girl approached, not completely sure what to do or what to say.

"What are you so shy about?" asked Williams, in his best baby voice. "Are you always this pretty, or only on Wednesdays?"

The girl smiled but didn't say a word. She was quickly followed by her father, a big man in a green parka.

"Are you going to call me pretty too?" he said to Tiger.

"No," Williams snapped back. "You're an ugly prick."

Everyone cracked up. Even the burly guy Williams had just insulted was in stitches. Williams could be rude, crude and outrageous at times, but the people here just loved it. They don't make hockey players like Tiger anymore, you could almost hear them say as they walked away. At every stop along the tour there would be a backlog at Tiger's stall where he would sit like Santa, waiting for the next child to be placed on his lap to have a picture taken with the famed hockey ruffian.

Gradually the lineup in the dressing room disappeared and the players had a few minutes by themselves before the second period began.

Mark Lofthouse began talking to a couple of players about his days in Washington under coach Tom McVie. After one particular game in which the opposing goalie made several saves with his pads stacked on top of one another, McVie decided to make a point in the next practice. He gathered the players around and blasted them for their inability to raise the puck over the goalie's pads the night before.

"So then McVie goes and lies in the goal crease," Lofthouse continued, incredulous even to this day at what he witnessed. "And all he has on is his track suit. Nothing else. Not a shred of equipment. And he says, 'Okay, I want everyone to come in and take a shot from the hash marks.' We're all looking at each other like he's nuts. We couldn't believe it. So we all start going in and shooting on him."

"Did anyone hit him?" someone asked.

"I think only one or two guys, but nothing serious."

Lofthouse remembered another time McVie wanted the players to practise breakaways. Ace Bailey, who would lose his life in the September 11 attacks, was a teammate of Lofthouse's at the time. Bailey often danced to his own music, and practices were no exception. Instead of trying to deke the goalie, he blasted a slapshot at him instead. McVie was furious at Bailey for not practising breakaways as instructed and suspended him for a few games.

"Ace was mad," Lofthouse remembered. "And if he could get back at you, he would. Well, the first game back after his suspension he scored a hat trick. It was almost like he did it to rub it in old Tom's face. Ace was something else."

Johnny Bower poked his head in the dressing room.

"Okay boys, it's time."

The Oldtimers headed out for the second period, which would go pretty much like the first. It didn't matter to the fans. It wasn't like they were expecting an upset. They were just happy to see Marcel Dionne make a no-look pass to Paul Reinhart sneaking in from the point. Or to watch Tiger ride his stick down the ice after scoring another goal.

After the game, the players changed and showered. Every game on the tour would be followed by a reception, where fans got another crack at getting autographs from the players and buying NHL memorabilia at a post-game auction. The players were handed beers as soon as they entered the banquet hall back at the High Country Inn, where the reception was being held. Hoggarth again served as the MC, introducing the players to polite applause from the hundred or so fans who had crowded into the room. The players had about twenty minutes to wolf down the plate of chicken wings and potato salad that was plopped down in front of them before people started filing by for autographs.

"I loved watching you play, Marcel," said one man.

"Thanks very much."

"Russ, it looks like you could still be playing," someone else said.

"Oh, I doubt that," Courtnall replied.

And so it went. Each fan had a connection with at least one of the players.

"I actually ran into you in a bar once, about fifteen years ago," someone said to Paul Reinhart.

"No kidding," Reinhart politely replied.

After dinner, the players began dispersing. Most were tired and were happy to head to their rooms after a long day. A few, however, including Williams and Russ Courtnall, headed to the hotel bar—the Yukon Mining Co.—for a nightcap. The Mining

Co. was a wonderfully eccentric little bar. The walls were made of corrugated plastic and were rolled up in the summer, when an outside deck allowed more than a hundred patrons to cram into the place. There were mining signs on the wall—"There are no four-legged animals in here, just the two-legged kind"—along with various kinds of mining tools and snowshoes and skis. The chairs were the plastic, lawn-furniture type, while the wooden tables were all painted hunter green. Along with the mining paraphernalia were Australian flags and rugby shirts, a nod to the heritage of the owner, who hailed from Down Under.

Tiger was joined in the bar by some old hunting buddies from the area. Courtnall also decided to sit down for a couple, as did Doug Bodger. But they wouldn't last nearly as long as Tiger and his friends, who would keep the bar open until five o'clock in the morning.

The next morning I met Wayne Babych for breakfast. Babych was one of those people who wore a perpetual smile. Nothing, it seemed, ever bothered him.

He was born and raised in Edmonton, the older brother by three years of Dave Babych, whose NHL career would far outlast his brother's. They were the product of hard-working Ukrainian parents—father, Edward, and mother, Tillie. Wayne and Dave played hockey almost every day of their young lives.

Wayne would play junior hockey in Portland and become one of the Western Hockey League's biggest stars. He ended up being the St. Louis Blues' first pick, third overall, in the 1978 entry draft. He played 67 games for the big club the following season, scoring 27 goals and 36 assists, and was just edged out for the Calder Trophy by Bobby Smith of the Minnesota North Stars.

Babych seemed to be a star in the making. He was big, powerful, fast and could put the puck in the net. He was paired with Bernie Federko and Brian Sutter when he first joined the Blues.

In his third year Red Berenson took over as coach and moved Babych to a line with Sweden's Jorgen Pettersson and Blake Dunlop. That year, Babych would score 54 goals and add 42 assists for 96 points. Suddenly, there wasn't a bigger star in St. Louis.

"It was awesome," Babych recalled. "I was treated so well in the bars you wouldn't believe it."

He was also offered a three-year contract for just under $300,000 U.S.—total. The deal included a $125,000 signing bonus and an option for a fourth year at $110,000. As it turned out, the Blues botched the language in the contract, and instead of having the option on the fourth year they ended up having to pick it up.

I had been told to ask Babych about his famous snipe hunt story. The Snipe Hunt was an occasional ritual that the Blues' veterans put rookies through. Babych had been warned by Harold Snepsts about the hunt before he got to St. Louis so that he wouldn't fall victim to it. Others wouldn't be so lucky. Like Jorgen Pettersson and defenceman Bill Stewart, a good Toronto kid.

"So what we did was tell Jorgen and Stewey that snipe hunting was a big thing in Missouri," Babych began. "Guys would be chatting about it in the dressing room, saying they had gone out hunting on the weekend and got so many snipe. Someone brought a fishing net to practice one day so Jorgen and Stewey could practice catching them. Someone would throw a pop can along the floor, that was supposed to be the snipe, and they'd have to try and snag it. It was hilarious watching them try.

"So anyway, the night arrives for the hunt. The whole team is going. Noel Picard (a former Blues player) owned a bar in Cuba, Missouri, not that far from St. Louis, and we all meet there first and have a few beers to get in the spirit. And we've got Jorgen and Stewey all primed up to go get their first snipe. Brian Sutter is one of the main ringleaders, and he's going to go with the rookies.

"So we go out to this field. We get Sutter to take them to this spot near this tree. Everyone else goes on the other side of this big bush, and we tell them that we're going to try and scare the snipe into the clearing so they can get them with their fishing nets. So we head off, and we've got beers, and we're just killing ourselves trying not to laugh out loud. It's dead silent out there. We're on about twenty acres. And we started saying things like, "There's one, there's one!" to get Jorgen and Stewey all excited that we actually see some.

"All of a sudden you hear the police sirens going and the lights are flashing, and there are cops everywhere. We just hide in our places. Meantime, Sutter takes off on Jorgen and Stewey and a cop goes after him faint-heartedly and comes back. The cops have got the rooks and they're armed and they're asking them if they realize that snipe hunting is illegal and that it's a federal offence that comes with a twenty-year jail sentence. They're laying it on real thick. We're listening to the whole thing, just cracking up. The cops are great. They handcuff them and throw them in the back of the police car. They're going to take them before a judge right away because of the seriousness of the crime."

Babych tears into a muffin and sips his coffee while he catches his breath.

"Okay, so we all know where they're being taken and show up at the courthouse. We've got the Blues in-house attorney in on it too. He's been called in to represent the players. We have a retired judge playing the role of the judge. Anyway, they bring poor old Jorgen and Stewey into the courtroom. They're looking real sad. Petrified. Anyway, the judge starts saying something and then our lawyer starts yakking and talking back and saying this is outrageous, and he gets thrown out of the courtroom. The bailiffs grab him and throw him out—the whole bit. It's beautiful. All of a sudden, Jorgen and Stewey are all on their own. Now they're really scared.

"Then the judge starts asking them questions about snipe hunting. He asks them about their nets. He gets the bailiff to measure their nets and says they're an illegal size. The judge then starts talking about deporting them because they're both foreigners, and suddenly Jorgen and Stewey are thinking their NHL careers are over. Jorgen starts crying. Stewey is as white as a sheet. The judge asks them if they want to make one call. They decide to call Emile Francis, who's the coach. Emile's been primed for the call. He gets on the line and the guys tell him what's happened. Emile just starts giving them shit: 'You guys should have known it was illegal. I don't care what you do you'd just better be at practice at nine sharp tomorrow morning or it's game over.' He slams the phone down.

"Now it's total panic. Hearing Francis screaming at them was the worst of all. They figure it's all over. They're told they're going to be taken to another jail, where they'll stay until a trial date is set. They're led off. The sheriff drives them around for about twenty minutes, it's dark and they don't have a clue where they are. Then he goes down this alley and backs up to the back door of this building. They think it's the jail. But it's Picard's bar in Cuba. When they walk through the door, we're all standing there waiting for them. The judge, our lawyer, everybody. Well, you should have seen their faces. They were the two happiest guys in the world at that moment. It was one of the all-time great scams when you think of how many people were involved to do it. It was amazing."

And maybe the best hockey story ever told.

After his fifty-four-goal campaign, Babych was looking forward to following it up with an equally impressive season. During a pre-season exhibition game, Babych—who could throw punches as well as anyone—dropped the gloves with Jimmy Mann, his future Oldtimers teammate who was then toiling for the Winnipeg Jets. Just as Babych was about to throw a punch the linesman grabbed his arm, ripping his rotator cuff. Babych went down in pain. He knew immediately something was very wrong.

He would never be the same.

Back then treatment for his kind of injury wasn't what it is today. Babych tried to play wearing a bulky harness on his shoulder that he had to strap on like a girdle. It only got worse. Then he took six weeks off trying to rehabilitate it the proper way. He ruined it for good when, in one of his first games back, he got in another fight. Doctors tried to take it apart and rebuild it, but it didn't work. Babych's production continued to decline, until finally he was put on waivers in 1984 and picked up by Pittsburgh.

Babych started out on a line with Mario Lemieux and Warren Young his first season as a Penguin. "I scored twenty and Young scored forty that year," Babych said. He even won the Emery Award for the best plus/minus average in the NHL. Still, Babych's injury prevented him from being the hockey player he once was. He bounced from Pittsburgh to a short stay in Quebec and finally to Hartford, where he was united with his brother Dave.

"Dave set me up for my first goal in Hartford," Babych recalled. "I went through some kind of hell in my career, but to play with my brother is all I wanted to ever do. From our days playing minor hockey together in Edmonton everything had come full circle. Now we were playing in the NHL together, which was always a dream of ours."

In a pre-season game in his second season with Hartford, Babych was playing alongside Ray Ferraro and Torrie Robertson when he received a two-handed slash across the side of the leg. Babych went down in a heap. The pain, he remembers to this day, was horrific. He couldn't get off the ice himself. The doctors checked him over and didn't like what they saw.

"I remember Emile Francis, who was the coach, coming to me with tears in his eyes to tell me I wouldn't have the use of my left leg again," Babych said. "I said I would. I had it operated on and I really worked hard to get mobile again. Anyway, I did it and ended up coming back to play the last four games of the season." The last four games of his NHL career.

Babych came back the following season, 1987, but his leg still hurt. During one particularly painful day at training camp, Wayne turned to his brother, Dave, and said it was over. He couldn't do it anymore. "I want to be able to walk when I'm older," he told his brother. "The doctors have said if I get another blow like the last one I may not walk again. It's not worth it, Dave." And he skated off the ice.

Babych would end up playing 519 regular-season games in the NHL. Unfortunately, it was just short of the number he needed for the NHL Players' Association bonus pension plan to kick in. "I thought Hartford might chip in the money to make up for it or somehow help me get the games as a gesture of appreciation, but they didn't," Babych said. "I had just got there, so there wasn't that history, I suppose."

After his career, Babych ran a water slide park in Winnipeg before getting into the golf business, building and operating a couple of courses with his brother. At forty-four, Babych was single and had no kids. Like any player who ever had the good fortune of wearing an NHL jersey, Babych cherished every game, every shift, every second he was on the ice.

"You just wish it could go on forever," he said before we asked for the bill. "It was the greatest time in my life. I just wish I could have played a little longer without a serious injury. It would have been interesting to see what I could have done."

We left our money. Gary Nylund and Russ Courtnall and a few of the others were wrapping up their breakfasts too. There was a plane to catch in an hour. It was on to Yellowknife.

"Remind me to tell you the story of the time I was pulled over by the cops in Pittsburgh and I was dressed as a streaker," Babych mentioned.

"Yep, I remember it like it was yesterday. Busy intersection. He asks me to get out and I've got this huge stuffed nylon strapped on as a dong and two tennis balls hanging underneath. And the cars are whizzing by honking their horns, screaming at me."

Babych shook his head.

"At least he didn't make me walk a straight line. That would have been really embarrassing."

CHAPTER 3

DYING IN YELLOWKNIFE

Steve Durbano was dying.

You could tell by the way he looked. His face had that horrible yellow tinge that death often sends in advance. It happens when your liver is shot from a lifetime of tequila shooters and whisky and sevens and a million beers. The pound of cocaine Durbano had sucked up his nose over the years didn't do his liver in, but it did help put him in jail; and that, as much as anything, had placed him in the horrible predicament he was in today.

"It's not good," Durbano said to his one-time adversary Tiger Williams in the Oldtimers dressing room before the game in Yellowknife.

"A year ago they gave me a year to live. I think I've got six months in me, and then I don't know."

"Are you still drinking?" Tiger asked him.

"You're damn right. I'm not going to sit on the couch and wait to die. If I want a beer I'm going to have a goddamn beer. I was

33

bad all of those years, so what do people think, all of a sudden I'm going to be God's Angel?"

"Ah, Durbie," said Williams. "You got to watch it, though."

"Ah, bullshit," Durbano shot back. "Not when you're dying, you don't."

If you followed the NHL in the 1970s you might remember Steve Durbano, mostly in connection with fights and penalties and a string of off-ice incidents. In six mostly forgettable years in the league, Durbano amassed more than one thousand minutes in penalties. And as his career swirled into the toilet, so did his life.

"It's too bad," said Williams, after Durbano left the room. "Because coming out of junior he wasn't a bad player. He was just a bad, bad drinker. And it will be the thing that ends up killing him."

Durbano was born and raised in Toronto, a tough kid from a solid middle-class family. He became a good enough hockey player to make the Toronto Marlboros. At 6'1" and 210 pounds, Durbano was a big blueliner by 1970s standards. He had a heavy shot and would get the odd point, but when he was on the ice the crowd would more likely end up cheering one of his fights than one of his goals. In his second year with the Marlies, Durbano picked up an amazing 371 penalty minutes, securing his reputation throughout the junior hockey world as one of the toughest customers around.

If you could control that fury, some NHL teams thought, you might have a solid defenceman one day. The New York Rangers, looking to add some toughness to its lineup, thought enough of Durbano's potential that the team made him a first-round draft choice in 1971, thirteenth overall. That year Durbano went ahead of future stars like Larry Robinson and Terry O'Reilly.

But before Durbano ever played a game for New York, he was traded to the St. Louis Blues. With St. Louis, Durbano showed he wasn't afraid to stand up to the toughest players in the league; but keeping up with the speed of the NHL game proved more challenging. Durbano struggled, and before his second season with the Blues was up he was traded to Pittsburgh, where he was hip-checked by Philadelphia's Andre "The Moose" Dupont in one game, fracturing his wrist in several places. It would never be the same and would be the reason, Durbano would say, he was out of the league four years later.

Midway through his third season with the Penguins, Durbano was traded to the Kansas City Scouts, the first and only NHL franchise in Kansas City. The Scouts' greatest accomplishment, as far as the record books went, was having the NHL's penalty-minutes leader on their team. That was Steve Durbano, who racked up 370 minutes in the box that season. (Of that total, 161 minutes were picked up in a Penguins uniform). Besides being known for having a short fuse on the ice, Durbano had a reputation as a loose cannon in the dressing room, too.

One story often told about Durbano was the time he didn't like what his coach was saying between periods, so he told him to get out of the room. When the coach didn't move fast enough, Durbano grabbed one of his skates that he'd taken off and fired it in the coach's direction. The skate missed the coach but the blade caught the dressing room door behind him, sticking into it much like an axe.

Durbano ended up in Colorado when the Scouts folded in Kansas City and became the Rockies in Denver. He would play alongside Dave Hanson, of *Slap Shot* fame, in Birmingham for the World Hockey Association for forty-five games in 1977 before his professional career wound up the following season in the city where it all began, St. Louis. In his final NHL season, Durbano played thirteen games, getting one goal, one assist and 103 penalty minutes.

Durbano was now standing beside the glass in the Yellowknife Community Arena watching Tiger Williams and the rest of the NHL Oldtimers play another team made up of local RCMP and firefighters. He was wearing blue jeans and a green parka and a hat that advertised a local tractor company. There was a sadness in his eyes. He took a swig from a can of apple juice that smelled of something else and then put it on the floor.

"What happened after your NHL career ended?" I asked Durbano, as we watched the Oldtimers warm up.

"What didn't happen," he said. "I had blown every cent I had when my career ended. I thought I'd have fourteen, fifteen years in the NHL and there would be plenty of time to save for the future. I was wrong."

Durbano had started dabbling in drugs as a young teenager in Toronto. It continued when he was in the NHL, where he suddenly had the money to buy more exotic drugs, like cocaine. Once he got a taste for cocaine, he couldn't get it up his nose fast enough. There were other drugs, which he mixed with booze to manufacture a lethal cocktail that began dragging him beneath the surface. Durbano once told a reporter that he tried to commit suicide five times during and after his hockey career because he was so depressed about his life.

One thing that ate away at Durbano was his failure to get any insurance money for the wrist injury he suffered and which he maintained put a premature end to his career. After his playing days were over, he hatched a crazy plan to sell drugs so that he could raise enough money to hire a lawyer and go after the insurance money he believed was rightly his.

By his own admission, Durbano made five trips to Bolivia to buy cocaine. Mostly, however, everything he bought down there for sale in North America ended up going up his nose and the noses of friends. He would end up making one trip too many and was nabbed at Lester B. Pearson International Airport in February 1981 for possessing five hundred grams of cocaine in the soles of his shoes.

He would end up serving just over two years of a seven-year sentence. Durbano told *The Hockey News* once that Ken Linesman, a linemate in Birmingham, was the only hockey player to visit him in prison.

Durbano would get in trouble with the law again in 1999, when he was found guilty of running an escort agency after he tried to hire an undercover policewoman he thought was a prostitute.

"After all that stuff, I just needed to get away," Durbano said in Yellowknife, puffing on a cigarette. "That's when I decided to head west. I visited my ex-wife and two teenaged daughters in Grande Prairie, Alberta, and ended up getting a job with a cleaning company that brought me up here."

And that is what he did now. Cleaned other people's carpets while waiting to die.

"This is the best thing that ever happened to me," Durbano said, as he continued to watch some of his old teammates on the ice. "I just wish I was going to have more time here. I have cancer of the liver and I have cirrhosis of the liver. I need a liver transplant, but I've been told that because of my past I'm not real high on the priority list. I'm not Mickey Mantle, in other words.

"A year ago they gave me a year to live. I think I've got six months in me, and then I don't know. I can feel it inside. I can feel the sickness in there. I can't describe it, but I have a whole bunch of tumors in there. A whole bunch of disease. I can feel them. I got this because of Hep C, and the way I got Hep C was because I was screwing around with drugs. So who do I have to blame? Nobody, that's right. So what do I have? I have memories of the past. That's it, memories."

Durbano picked up his can of juice and whatever else it had in it and took another long rip on it. Some snuck out of the side of his mouth and dribbled down his chin.

The first period of the game ended with the Oldtimers up by four goals. In the room, the players took their helmets off and loosened their skates, waiting for their fans—the lucky program holders from Yellowknife—to start filing in for autographs.

"Did I tell you about the time Durbano's wife slugged me?" Tiger said to me.

"No."

"Oh, yeah," he continued. "Steve and I got into it one night and I went to the penalty box, and this woman starts screaming at me. Well, the glass wasn't nearly as high around the penalty box then as it is now and she wound up with her purse and just corked me one right in the head. I swear it was the hardest I've ever been hit. I don't know what she had in that thing, maybe rocks, but she nearly knocked me out."

Around the room, the guys were talking about the best skaters they played against. Someone said Gilbert Perreault. "He had a move where he could change directions in a split second on one foot," said Marcel Dionne. Mario Lemieux, everyone seemed to agree, was deceptively fast. And Guy Lafleur was awfully hard to catch if he got in front of you.

Gary Nylund, meantime, was fiddling with his helmet. While the shell wasn't the same one he used in the NHL, the inside foam padding was. You could still read the now-faded words Nylund had written on the padding for inspiration. Confidence, Hard Work, Determination. Or, as Nylund said laughing, "all that bullshit I used to believe in."

The game unfolded much like the first one, the Oldtimers goals coming in bunches. Tiger got a couple. Mark Lofthouse got a couple. And Wayne Babych too. Russ Courtnall whirled around the ice, untouchable, even by the most gifted players on the other team. He toyed with them all, not much interested in scoring but in setting up his teammates with deft passes, no-look rockets that somehow found their way through a crowd of players onto the stick of Dionne, or Rouse or Reinhart, who liked sneaking in from the point.

This wasn't the NHL, but as far as fine hockey went, it was as good as it got for the people of Yellowknife. There was plenty of oohing and aahing. You could see parents pointing out certain players to their children. You could imagine what they were saying: the time they saw Dionne score three goals in Vancouver and Tiger go toe-to-toe with Terry O'Reilly.

Yellowknife could be a wonderful town to visit. In the summer. Located on the edge of the Precambrian Shield, a fact that Tiger Williams whipped out before we had even touched down here, the Yellowknife countryside is dotted with hundreds of lakes, which boast some of the best fishing anywhere in North America. The streets of the city are filled with history. You can take a walk through Willow Flats, down on the shore of Yellowknife Bay, and stumble upon Ragged Ass Road, named for a now-abandoned mine north of the city. Replica Ragged Ass Road street signs have become a popular souvenir. If you wander down Franklin Avenue, through the Peace River Flats on Back Bay, you can also find another famous local street, Lois Lane. Yellowknife is the home town of Margot Kidder, the actress who brought Lois Lane to life on the big screen.

But Yellowknife is really to be enjoyed in the summer months. Wintertime, when temperatures regularly plummet to minus forty, is a different story. The outdoor thermometer atop one downtown building the day we arrived heralded a temperature of minus twenty-two. It felt colder.

The historic downtown core was a depressing collage of greys and browns. The streets were filled with slush and the exhaust fumes from ubiquitous half-tonne trucks. People walked determinedly along the sidewalks, anxious, it appeared, to get inside, anywhere, as quickly as possible.

"Our winters may be long, but we enjoy more frost-free days a year than Calgary!" a tourist brochure proclaimed. You wondered how many new citizens that discovery drew to the area. Not as many, it was certain, as the recent discovery of diamonds north of here, which had caused a boom that now rivalled the early days of the gold rush, locals insisted. Yellowknife's population was now back over eighteen thousand, although it was hard to tell because people spent as little time as possible outside at this time of year.

After the game, the players returned to the hotel for another post-game banquet and autograph session. It was funny how people acted around celebrities. Even old celebrities. As the room began to fill up you could see people pointing at this player and that player, you could see others dying to go up and ask for an autograph but not being able to summon up the nerve. When food arrived for the team, it seemed like another obstacle for those autograph seekers anxious to get Johnny Bower's or Paul Reinhart's or Russ Courtnall's name on a glossy picture they carried with them.

The stop in Yellowknife marked an important date for one member of the tour. It was Johnny Bower's birthday. He was seventy-seven. On the flight from Whitehorse, the crew presented the Leafs legend with a birthday cake. Being the most modest man in the world, he shook his head while carefully balancing the cake on his lap.

"Why did you do that? I don't need a cake. Come, everyone, and get some of this."

Bower smiled, his eyes crinkling up under his big round glasses. We all smiled back, from the most jaded and cynical among us, like Tiger, to Paul Reinhart, who regarded Bower with the awe of a child. For all he himself had accomplished in hockey, Reinhart looked across the aisle of the plane and still couldn't believe that he was in the company of the legendary Leafs goalie. It would be the highlight of his trip.

Ron Hoggarth, who was at the microphone, urged the crowd that had gathered at the Yellowknife reception to help sing "Happy Birthday" to Johnny. The crowd and players all joined in, while the object of all the attention bowed his head—uncomfortable, it seemed, in the spotlight. After "Happy Birthday" was finished, Hoggarth asked Bower to come to the microphone and say a few words. Johnny began by saying thanks and, perhaps feeling buoyed by the warm feeling in the room, recalled when he did a little singing himself once. While playing for the Leafs he'd made a recording of "Honky, the Christmas Goose," and the proceeds from the sale of the record went to charity.

"Now let's see if I still remember the words," he said.

Honky, Honky the Christmas Goose
Got so fat that he was no use
'Til he learned how to blow his nose
And honk the way a Goose nose blows.

After that and just for fun, it was a simple matter
He would blow his honky horn, to see the people scatter
Cars and planes and trucks and trains would get out of
*   his way*
And when they heard the honky horn, this is what they'd say!

Ohhhhhhhh . . . Honky, Honky the Christmas Goose
Got so fat that he was no use
'Til he learned how to blow his nose
And honk the way a Goose nose blows.

The crowd loved it and gave Bower the kind of ovation usually reserved for shutouts and first-star selections. Johnny seemed happy with himself and returned to his seat, getting taps on the back from the players as he passed them.

"Johnny is amazing," said Jimmy Mann as he sat in his chair, sipping on a beer.

This was one of the few times on the tour that Mann could relax. For a few minutes after dinner. Because he was an employee of Xentel, he had responsibilities on the tour that the other players didn't. He was to make sure all the equipment got packed up and loaded in vans for transport to our plane. He let all the players know what time they were to meet in the hotel lobby before games and in the morning for the bus to the airport. He made sure everyone had a hotel room.

Mann was a big guy, whose life on the road with the Old-timers had taken a toll on his fitness. Still, he would be the only player to lace them up in every game on all four of the tours. But that also meant months of late nights and early mornings, deep-fried food and frosted mugs of beer.

He had hands the size of shovels. The knuckles of his left one were lined with dozens of white scars that look like spider veins. When it came to punching people, Mann was all southpaw. And, like Steve Durbano before him, Jimmy Mann had only one role in the National Hockey League.

Fighter.

Mann was born in Verdun, an area that had produced Denis Savard and Scotty Bowman. His dream was to play major junior somewhere in the province. Mann played with Mike Bossy in Laval before being traded to Sherbrooke.

He scored 35 goals and added 47 assists his last season with the Beavers. He also had 260 minutes in penalties, 17 minutes shy of his previous season's total. Yes, Jimmy Mann could score goals, but he was a fighter first, who ruled the roost in his last year of junior. At 6'1" and 210 pounds, Mann had that combination of size and toughness mixed with some skill that appealed to someone like John Ferguson, who built an NHL career on much the same foundation.

When it came time for Winnipeg to make its first selection in the 1979 NHL entry draft, Ferguson, the Jets' GM at the time, chose Mann. While Mann was Ferguson's type of player, history would not be kind to the selection; the Jets passed over future NHL stars like Mark Messier, Glenn Anderson and Kevin Lowe, who were all still available when it was Winnipeg's turn to pick. But then, Ferguson wasn't the only GM who missed the boat in that regard.

"The first year I made $65,000 and got an $80,000 signing bonus," said Mann, leaning back in his chair. "I went out and bought a brand new Trans-Am. A real muscle car. It was red. I gave my parents $15,000 so they could buy a new car too. My dad, Donald, was a construction worker who never missed a game of mine. He would drive me everywhere. When I was playing junior, we'd get back at three or four o'clock in the morning from road games and my dad would have to drive a few hours to come and pick me up at that hour. He'd take me home and then he'd go to work. He never said boo about it. Never complained. He just shut his mouth and watched the games. My mom, Marjorie, on the other hand, was always too nervous to watch."

One time, Marjorie Mann decided to summon up the nerve to go watch her son play in Sherbrooke. As they arrived for the game, she and Donald noticed police cars everywhere. As it happened, a brawl between the two teams had broken out during the pre-game warmup, and the police had to be called in to help break it up. Once Marjorie got inside to see her son in the thick of it, she couldn't watch. She went to the bathroom and got sick. The police eventually sorted things out on the ice, and the game went ahead.

By his final year of junior, Mann recalled, he was hated by many coaches. At least one would hire tough guys from recreational leagues—pure goons, who could barely skate—just to face off against Mann. "This one guy would pay these morons a hundred dollars to fight me. But it was so stupid. By my last year in the league, because of the reputation I had built up, I hardly had to do anything. It was all intimidation by then. I'd look at some guy and say, 'You touch the puck and I'll cut your head off.' I had all the room in the world out there."

The NHL was a different story. Although Mann was still considered tough, there were lots of players who could match his meanness.

Ferguson made it clear to Mann that he wasn't in Winnipeg

to be the team's leading scorer. He was there to protect the "skilled" players—the ones who were paid big money to score. If the Jets got behind early in a game, Mann's job was to give his team a boost by jumping someone on the other team and laying a beating on him. And that became Jimmy Mann's life. He was an attack dog whose heart sped up and blood raced when he hit the ice because he knew that in minutes the crowd would be screaming and he would be trading punches with someone. It was the kind of job that could wear on a person after a while.

"My first game against Boston," Mann was saying, putting down his beer. "I remember I fought Terry O'Reilly, Al Secord and Stan Jonathan in three consecutive shifts. You knew that it was expected. That's all I did after a while, and I hated it. I wasn't used to just fighting and not playing any kind of role in terms of scoring or helping the team offensively. And once you have that kind of reputation in the league, it's almost impossible to get rid of it. You're a goon forever."

"Were you ever scared of anyone?" I asked Mann.

"I was nervous," he said. "But never scared. If you were scared, you were done. I knew that. You have to think you can beat up anybody. You have to play on the edge the entire time, and when you play on the edge you can lose it sometimes, and I lost it. I mean, I had a bad temper too, and when you combine that with the way I was conditioned to play, I would just snap."

"What would happen?"

"Oh, I'd jump into the penalty box to go after somebody. Especially if someone got the best of me in a fight. You know that your reputation is at stake. Your job is on the line too. I felt like I was literally fighting for a job every night. Fergie (John Ferguson) used to say at training camp, 'See that guy over there? He wants your job this year. And that's how it was when I played. I felt if I didn't do well then they'd start looking around at other people to do the same thing. And that became an exhausting way to live after a while. Against certain teams, the tough ones like Philly or the Bruins, I couldn't sleep at night because I knew I'd have to fight a lot. Those teams had four or five guys who could really go, and the Jets had me, basically, that was it. The older I got, the harder it became to get ready for those games. And I knew that unless I was completely, one hundred per cent, ready to fight, I could get really hurt out there."

As I listened to Mann talk, it was hard not to feel sorry for the guy. Which, I know, was an odd emotion to have for someone who was your common-variety thug for his entire career. But then, that was the job that was vacant. Thug. And when he played, NHL teams posted those kinds of positions. If you were a player like Jimmy Mann, and the dream of your entire life was to play in the NHL, then you did what you had to do to reach that dream. Even if it meant feeling sick before games because you knew what lay ahead.

The low point of Mann's career would actually take place during his second year in the league. It happened, in fact, on January 13, 1982, during a game between the Jets and the Pittsburgh Penguins. The Penguins were losing to the Jets 6–1 late in the game. Pittsburgh forward Paul Gardner had scored his team's lone goal.

Gardner was talking to Winnipeg defenceman Dave Babych about nothing when he got clobbered from behind. It was Mann. The Jets tough guy sucker-punched Gardner twice. The blows were spectacularly powerful and destructive, breaking Gardner's jaw right off its hinges. When he went to the hospital for treatment, emergency room doctors said the damage was worse than that suffered by a victim in a bad car accident.

As it happened, there was an official from the provincial attorney general's office in the crowd that night. Mann was charged with assault by Attorney General Roland Penner. He would eventually plead guilty and be fined five hundred dollars.

"It was bad," Mann admitted nineteen years later. "It was one of those things where it all was like a blur. I was twenty-one years old at the time. Gardner had cross-checked one of our players across the face, and so I went out to take care of it. It's funny, though. My first year, I had a rookie card that was sold and had the fact that I was the NHL penalty-minutes leader (287 PIMS). The second year, I had a card too. I never had another card after that, and I played seven more seasons. Alan Eagleson was Paul Gardner's agent at the time, and I think he blackballed me."

Mann liked playing for Ferguson because he always knew where he stood: if Mann wasn't fighting enough, Fergie would let him know. If he had a particularly successful night at the fights, Fergie would come around his stall after the game to tap Mann on the shoulder and say, "Good job." Coming from a legendary tough guy like Ferguson, this meant a lot to Mann. But Mann also saw another side of Ferguson that wasn't as pleasant. He had a temper that was deadly.

Mann recalled one day during the 1983–84 season when defenceman Bryan Maxwell was with the Jets. After one particular game in which Ferguson saw something he didn't like, he suggested during practice the next day that Maxwell wasn't being a team player. But if anyone was a team player it was Maxwell, who was loved in the dressing room. He was furious at Ferguson for singling him out but mostly for suggesting that he was putting himself before his teammates. Maxwell decided to go and see Ferguson and give him a piece of his mind, ignoring pleas from his teammates to not do it.

After the meeting, Maxwell walked into the trainer's room, where a few guys were sitting around getting treatment. Maxwell pulled up a chair and was beginning to tell the guys about his meeting. He barely got started when the door opened with a loud bang. It was Ferguson, and there was smoke and fire and all-out fury in his eyes as he marched towards Maxwell. Mann was sitting nearby.

"You son of a bitch," Ferguson said to Maxwell as he grabbed him by the shirt.

It looked like Ferguson was going to smack his player when Mann and another player grabbed their GM.

"You'll never play here again," Ferguson shouted at Maxwell as he got dragged away. "You're done!"

The door to the trainer's room was made out of cheap pressboard plywood. Ferguson slammed it shut behind him. Seconds later there was another crash, and all of a sudden Mann, Maxwell and the others saw Ferguson's shoe appear through the door. In his rage he had apparently kicked the door a little too hard, putting a hole right through it.

"The best part," Mann said, recalling the day, "was that he couldn't get his foot back out. You could see him wiggling it and trying to get it back through the door, but he couldn't. It was hilarious. Eventually he got it out."

And Bryan Maxwell was put on waivers by Ferguson and claimed by the Pittsburgh Penguins.

Hockey players are notorious pranksters, but rare was the player who ever tried pulling something on Ferguson. Mann felt no such compunction.

As he sat around the banquet room in Yellowknife, Mann remembered one flight to Toronto during which he decided to give his teammates a little laugh. Ferguson always sat at the front of the plane. Quite often he would doze off, and then just before landing he would wake up and go to the washroom to make sure his hair was perfectly coiffed and his tie was perfectly straight. John Ferguson always wanted to look good.

"So he's asleep, and I get some shaving cream," Mann began as he laughed at the memory. "It's the real foamy stuff. I give it a shake and load 'er up pretty good on Fergie's head. I figure he'll go to the washroom like he always does, and he'll discover it before he leaves the plane. Sure enough, he gets up and goes to the washroom. Everyone is looking at him, barely able to contain themselves. Well, the washrooms on the plane—it was a DC-9, I'll always remember—are real tiny, and Fergie can barely fit in it.

"A few minutes later he comes out, and lo and behold, the shaving cream is still on his head. Everyone's looking at one another. We figure he didn't bend down enough in front of the mirror to see the shaving cream. Now no one wants to say anything to him. Everyone is too afraid. The plane lands, and Fergie gets off and starts walking through the airport with this stuff still on his head. We're just killing ourselves. Finally, someone says something to him, and he goes to a washroom and gets it off and doesn't say a word. Nothing."

A week later the Jets were on the road, and in one city Mann purchased an expensive pair of cowboy boots. "They cost me four hundred dollars U.S., which was a fortune at the time." The Jets returned to Winnipeg and a few days later were getting ready to hit the road again, this time in always-soggy Vancouver. While the players were on the ice practising, Ferguson showed up and stood at the bench talking to some of the players. "Hey, Jimmy," Ferguson shouted to Mann. "Make sure you don't get your feet wet in Vancouver. It rains a lot there, remember." Mann couldn't figure out what Ferguson was talking about. Watch his feet? It rains a lot? He put it out of his mind and finished the practice.

After it was over, the players filed into the dressing room. Mann headed to his stall. After a few minutes he realized his new cowboy boots weren't anywhere to be seen. He looked around and spotted his boots on a bench across the room. He went over to get them, but when he went to lift them up he couldn't. Mann quickly discovered why. Someone had put several heavy-duty four-inch nails right through the boot and the top of the bench, and then banged the nail sideways on the other side. Mann had to get a hacksaw and cut right through the boot to get them off the bench.

Fergie had exacted his revenge.

The 1983–84 season would be Mann's last as a Jet. In February, he was traded to Quebec for the Nordiques' fifth-round pick in that year's draft. Mann's career was on a downward spiral. Injuries were taking their toll on his ability to fight. After his infamous rookie season, in which he racked up 287 minutes in penalties, his numbers began to fall. The following season, split between the NHL and the minors, his big-league penalty minutes total was 105, then 79 the following season and 73 after that. In his last year with Winnipeg he actually spent time back in Sherbrooke, playing in the American Hockey League with the Jets' farm team, also called the Jets.

"It was nice to go back there, but I still wanted to play in the NHL," said Mann. "I still could play."

Mann missed the entire 1986–87 season with an abdominal injury, which he had originally suffered in 1984. The following season, Quebec set him free. Mann thought that was it, the end of his career. He was going to be a cop, he had decided. Then, out of the blue, he got a call from the Pittsburgh Penguins, who were looking for some protection for Mario Lemieux. Mann thought hard about it. Did he have it in him? Could he still play the role the teams wanted him to play? Did he have it in his fists? More importantly, did he have it in his heart?

Mann decided to take the Penguins up on their tryout offer. After all, how could he pass up a chance to play with one of the best players in the world? Mann arrived at training camp and immediately faced hostilities. Pittsburgh had three tough guys in its organization, and one of the three thought the job of enforcer for the upcoming season was his. Then Mann shows up.

"It even started in the hotel," Mann recalled, shaking his head at the thought. "These tough guys would try and stare me down in the lobby. I say to them, 'What are you looking at? Screw you, asshole.' Now this is without a word of a lie. I went to training camp, and the first day on the ice, on my first shift, I had four fights. The same shift, four fights. Guys were coming off the bench to fight me. I was just dead after the last one. I had nothing left. Pierre Creamer was the coach then. He said, 'Jimmy, you're done for the day. Good job.' I said, 'No problem.'"

The season had barely got underway when Mann broke his elbow. That was it. Nine games playing on the same team as Mario Lemieux. Still, Mann figured, that wasn't bad for a goon from Quebec, playing alongside the greatest player his home province had ever produced. Mann played ten games in the International Hockey League that year with the Muskegon Lumberjacks. The following year, he played thirty-eight games for the Indianapolis Ice, also of the IHL. During that brief time, he compiled an amazing 275 minutes in penalties, but he had had enough. He wanted to go home.

His wife would come down from Quebec to watch him play twice a month during his last season as a professional hockey player. During his thirty-eighth game, Mann got into a fight his first shift and was thrown out of the game. His back was sore, his hands were sore. His heart was no longer in it. He walked away that day and never returned.

Mann finished his beer and leaned on the table. The players were starting to leave. Most of the fans were still around, hoping to get a few minutes of conversation with some of the players to go with their autographs.

CHAPTER 4

THE MAD TRAPPER

O F ALL THE STOPS on our northern tour, Inuvik was the one the players seemed most excited about.

Except for the guys who had played there on previous Oldtimers tours—guys like Tiger and Marcel and Jimmy Mann—none of us had ever been this close to the Arctic circle. For most players, cities like Edmonton, which they had visited during their NHL playing days, marked the farthest north they had ever been.

As we approached the town by air early one morning, it was quickly apparent this wasn't Timmins or Prince George or Fort McMurray. This was the *far* north, with a lonely, almost tortuous terrain all its own. It was probably spectacular in the summer, but in November the area's famous tundra was covered in snow.

Tiger was a frequent visitor to these parts, a serious hunter who once bagged two enormous muskox using a bow and arrow as powerful as a shotgun. "Maybe I'll slip out and bag another one while we're here," he snorted.

After we landed, the team jumped into a couple of waiting vans. Tiger was in ours and acted as tour guide for the ten-minute ride into town. Inuvik, he began to inform us, had some of the worst conditions in the world for building. Not just because the temperature could plunge to fifty below zero, which could make driving nails kind of difficult, but because of the permafrost underlying the entire area. When the permafrost thawed in the summer, the ground could shift dramatically and buildings could crumble. So, he informed us, most of the buildings and homes in the town sat above ground on pilings, stilt-like poles made of wood and in some cases steel, that were drilled through the active layer of permafrost into the continuous layer of permafrost underneath. In between the ground floor of a building was a crawl space, which was needed to direct building heat away from the ground.

"What they had to do to build this place is absolutely amazing, when you think of it," Tiger said, as we all looked out the window at the whiteness.

The airport we had just landed on, for instance, had a six-thousand-foot runway that was built on pads six-feet deep in some cases. Still, there were dramatic examples of the best efforts of construction crews not being a match for Mother Nature. In one case, a fifty-foot section of road suddenly dropped twenty-five feet when the ice below it melted.

Inuvik is located two degrees above the Arctic Circle on the Mackenzie River and Delta. It sits between treeless tundra and the northern boreal forest. If we had flown in during the summer months, we would have seen the spectacular maze of lakes and streams of the Mackenzie Delta.

"What the hell do people do up here?" someone in the back of the van asked.

"Hunt, fish," he said. "And it's still a government town. Well, sort of."

Someone else mentioned that Inuvik had more than thirty taxis—the most per capita of any city in North America.

"It's true," our driver insisted.

For most of its existence, Inuvik was in every sense a no-man's land that sat between areas occupied by the Inuit to the north and the Dene to the south. Occasionally it would be visited by the odd trapper. But in the 1950s the Canadian government felt there was a need for a regional administrative centre in the Western Arctic, and Inuvik was chosen as the site.

In the mid-1980s the government decided to close the Canadian Forces Base here, and seven hundred people fled town. Over the years oil and gas exploration had brought work, but that was never something the town could count on. Today, the population of Inuvik hovered around three thousand, mostly native, living an often-forlorn existence. Some of the locals made a living running tourist gift shops and craft stores. There were hotels and motels and restaurants. And many area residents made a living as guide outfitters for tourists interested in hunting and fishing. But that was mainly a summertime operation. Many people subsisted on welfare, and as with many communities in the far north, alcohol abuse was a serious problem, as was violence.

As we approached the town we could see one of its few landmarks, the famous Igloo Church. Actually, it shares the same name as the famous Notre Dame cathedral in Paris—Our Lady of Victory Church. But to almost everyone, it is known as the Igloo Church because it was built and designed in 1958 by volunteers to resemble an igloo. It is marked by a nine-foot-high cross on its top.

We were staying at the Eskimo Inn, which sat right across from the Mad Trapper Pub, where a steady stream of patrons staggered in and out.

Most of us were hungry and anxious to try whatever constituted local fare. After finding our rooms and getting rid of our luggage, most of us gathered in the downstairs restaurant of the Eskimo Inn. Nearly all went for the $7.95 Bison Burger, which we later agreed was excellent.

Any time the guys sat down, even without beers, it became story time. This didn't happen by design, it just happened, and it seemed as natural as taking a breath. You'd sit down and then someone would begin.

"Did Russ tell you the story about the night Rick Vaive got his 'C' ripped off his jersey?" Nylund began, looking at me.

"No."

And Nylund was off. As it turned out, the story wasn't as much about Leafs coach Dan Maloney's decision to strip Vaive of the captaincy as it was about him wanting to kill Courtnall later that night.

"What happened was, the night Vaive got stripped of the 'C' we all went out drinking," Nylund said. "And there was an eleven o'clock curfew or something. Anyway, Borje Salming is telling people not to worry about the curfew, we'd already missed it anyway, and having a few more beers wouldn't hurt anything.

"Anyway, Russ hangs in for a few more and just as he gets back to his room, there's a knock on the door. It's Maloney, and he's doing a curfew check. Well, Russ hops under the covers in his clothes. He's rooming with Brad Smith at the time, Motor City Smitty. Well, Smitty decides he's not going to let Maloney in the room to check. He says Courtnall is there, not to worry. Well, Maloney wants to see for himself and is convinced Russ is still out and wants to kill him.

"Well, Smitty and Maloney get into it in the doorway. Smitty doesn't have a shirt on and they're going at it. Maloney had this pen in his hand that he was using to do roll call with, and he's raking Smitty's chest with it. Anyway, Maloney never does get into the room. The next day at practice, we see Smitty's chest and there's all these red marks, like he's been scratched by a cat. I asked him what the hell happened, and he said he'd got into it with Maloney. I asked him who won, and Smitty said: 'I owned him when I played against him and I owned him last night.'"

Everyone laughed hysterically. But the incident, Nylund and Courtnall both suggested, said it all about the Leafs' problems at the time. For most of the early 1980s the team was in complete chaos and disarray. Both Nylund and Courtnall had arrived on the Leafs with great expectations, thrilled about being part of arguably the most famous hockey franchise in the NHL. They were both aware that the Leafs had not been a powerhouse in years, but they were anxious to be part of a turnaround.

"It was sad," Nylund said. "There just wasn't any leadership. I remember one game—I don't know who we were playing, but we were getting thumped and we went into the dressing room between periods and I started screaming that we had to get going, that we stunk and we were embarrassing ourselves. And I'll never forget it, there was Bill Derlago, sitting in the corner with his legs crossed, smoking a cigarette. In the dressing room! And he says, 'Yea, guys let's get going. This is bullshit.' But that was what it was like. That was the kind of leadership we had then."

After lunch I went for a brief walk around town. I returned to my room and began thinking about the game that night. I was getting surprisingly nervous.

It had nothing to do with the fact the arena would be sold out. So what if there were fifteen hundred strangers watching? That wasn't it at all. At the root of my feelings, I quickly surmised, was this gnawing doubt. What if I couldn't keep up? What if every pass from the former NHLers bounced off my stick and into the hands of the enemy? What if the opposition was really good and my team needed a real contribution from me? The reality was, I couldn't skate like I used to. And I wasn't nearly in the kind of shape I had been in even a few years earlier. What if I completely embarrassed myself?

By the time I arrived at the Midnight Sun recreation arena, some of the players were already starting to get dressed. A few were still laughing over a story that Jimmy Mann had just finished telling. Mann was in Quebec toiling on the bench and in the press box mostly for the Nordiques and their coach, Michel Bergeron. During one game Mann had again been relegated to the role of bystander, sitting in the middle of the bench watching his teammates on either side get regular shifts. In the course of the game, a couple of defencemen had gone down with injuries.

At one point during the third period, Bergeron told Mann to go and sit at the end of the bench with the defencemen. "Hey, this is great," Mann remembered thinking. "I'm going to play some defence. This should be fun." Mann got to the end of the bench and looked to Bergeron for further instruction. "I want you to work the gate because we're short D-men and our guys are going to be coming off and on real fast," Bergeron told Mann. The Nordiques' tough guy was stunned for a second. "Screw you," he told his coach and moved back to his old spot on the bench.

All the guys were now in the room. It was time to start giving it to the rookie.

"You mess up once and you're done," Tiger said, with approving nods from the rest of the team.

"If you can't keep up, get off the ice and take your stuff off because you're not here to embarrass us," he kept going. "And remember, nobody is here to see you. You're a nobody. We're the stars. They paid to see us, not you. So you get the puck, you look to set one of us up."

It was hard to know if Williams was serious or not. He was good at keeping a straight face while making the most ludicrous comments. But if he was trying to make me even more nervous than I already was, he was doing a good job.

After he was finished with me, Williams began telling the

room the story of the charity game he played in against a bunch of Hollywood types in Saskatoon. The game was being held to raise money for one of Gordie Howe's charities, and Mr. Hockey himself was there to drop the puck. Sometime during the first period, Williams was telling the guys, he ran actor Jason Priestley face-first into the boards. Priestley failed to see the humour in Williams's shot and left the ice in a huff.

During the first intermission, organizers from Team Hollywood let it be known that they weren't coming back on the ice unless Williams was gone. "Some guy, I think it was Priestley's agent or something, he comes and tells our guy, 'Doesn't Tiger Williams understand these people make their living from their faces?' They even went to Gordie and tried to get him to kick me off the ice, but he apparently said no. Anyway, they ended up letting me play—but that little suck Priestley didn't come near me the entire night."

In ten minutes we would be going out for the pre-game warm-up. I tightened my skates as the screeching sound of sock tape being wrapped around hockey socks filled the room. I recalled the spring when I first laced up my skates with the Oldtimers and I was just about to head out on the ice for introductions. I began looking around for my gloves, which I had put on a shelf above my locker stall. Suddenly they were nowhere to be found. "Two minutes," someone said. Where were my gloves? Finally it dawned on me to look in my hockey bag. There they were, wrapped into tiny balls by what appeared to be ten rolls of tape. I frantically looked for the start of the end of the roll to start peeling it off. When I couldn't find it, I just grabbed a piece and started pulling violently. I looked up to see a few of the players watching me; they were in hysterics. I finally managed to get the tape off, literally seconds before I was to be introduced.

Back in Inuvik, meantime, we skated on to the ice for the warm-up, slowly turning in circles, taking the odd shot on goal.

Eventually Richard Brodeur got between the pipes, and we whistled shots at him. Each time we skated near the red line, I instinctively looked at our competition, which was warming up at the other end.

Williams had told us about a player on the other team named Timmy Gordon, a local First Nations kid who was apparently quite a player. A few years earlier, Williams had the Canucks take a look at him. They liked what they saw enough to give him a shot in the minors. But after a few weeks away from Inuvik, Gordon got homesick. He tried to play hockey in Germany later, but the same thing happened. A different culture, language, people, was just too much for Gordon, so he returned to Inuvik, where he now worked cleaning apartments.

He was easy to spot. He was Number 10, the fastest guy on the ice next to Russ Courtnall.

Warm-up wrapped up, and we went to the dressing room while the ice was cleaned. My teammates began offering last-minute advice, most of it sincere. "When you're looking for a pass, make sure your stick is on the ice," said Gary Nylund. "When we're down at their end, try and get in front of the net and we'll try and hit you," said Bob Rouse. I took a sip of bottled water and tried to calm down.

Don Jackson, the former world champion figure skater who was on the tour as part of the intermission entertainment, popped his head in the room. "Okay guys, they're ready." Which was the signal to get ready for the flashy introductions that preceded each game. I was also dreading this. What were they going to say about me? "He once scored the winning goal in a house league game in his second year of atom. Now he occasionally plays with some cranberry farmers on Wednesday nights. Please welcome . . . Gary Mason!" And everyone would start looking at one another and begin scratching their head and there might be, I even imagined, a few boos. "Who invited him?" I could hear someone yell.

Then, when I discovered who I would be following in the introduction lineup—Marcel Dionne and Tiger Williams—I felt even worse. I tried to comfort myself with the knowledge that it would all be over in a few seconds and then hopefully people would forget and not ask for their money back. Before I knew it, Dionne was being introduced, his long list of Hall of Fame accomplishments being loudly applauded as he skated onto the ice. Next, the public address announcer began reciting Williams's colourful NHL career, and he skated onto the ice amid of blaze of laser lights. It was my turn.

"He works for the Providence newspaper and he's writing a book . . . please welcome Gary Mason!"

Wha, wha, wha . . . what? I worked for what newspaper? And he's writing a book? Could they have made me appear any more irrelevant, meaningless, any more like a tiny speck of dust that had no business on the ice with these guys? And what was "the Providence newspaper?" Did they mean the *Province* newspaper, which was the other daily newspaper in Vancouver? The competition? I worked for the *Vancouver Sun*. As I went down the line of my teammates, punching their gloves until I arrived at the end of the line, I tried to put it out of my head. I could tell that my teammates were enjoying the moment and that I would hear about it later.

I would be spelling Jimmy Mann off on right wing on a line with Marcel Dionne and Wayne Babych. After a couple of shifts Mann told me to go on for him, and I headed out on the fly when Mark Lofthouse came to the bench for a change. Our defencemen had the puck and I moved to my wing. Thirty seconds into my shift, I somehow found myself with the puck about twenty feet in front of the other team's goalie and under a pretty good head of steam. I could also see a defenceman approaching fast from my left, so I decided to let a hard wrist shot fly to the goalie's blocker side.

You could have heard the clang all the way over in Tuktoyak-tuk. I had the goalie beat, but the puck clanged off the post and into the corner. I looked around to see my teammates on the bench hitting each other, laughing at my bad break. As it turned out, it was the best scoring chance I had all night. I would have two or three more glorious scoring opportunities but fail to capitalize, as they say on *Hockey Night in Canada*. One time I shot wide, and another I partially fanned on. I did, however, manage to help set up a few goals in that first period and went to the dressing room a healthy plus-3.

The boys gave it to me pretty good about the post. And the fanned shot that followed shortly after. And, of course, someone had to bring up my famous introduction. "What was that?" said Doug Bodger, to hoots from my teammates. "'And he's writing a book'? A book on what? Whales? The stars? Pornography?" Bodger even had me laughing after a while.

Soon the lucky program winners began filing into the room, and the nightly procession began. Because I was playing, my autograph was being sought too. The programs contained a centre pullout section of pictures of all the players in the form of hockey cards that the kids could pull out. Mine, of course, was not among them, a point I would have to make continually to the steady stream of six- and seven- and eight-year-olds popping up in front of me, bundled up in their winter coats, some with little pens in their hands. I felt like a bit of an imposter, but I figured if I scribbled really quickly the kids wouldn't know whose signature it was anyway. If I wrote "Gary Mason" nice and clearly, they'd wonder later who the hell Gary Mason was. Then they'd have to ask their parents, who took them to the game, who Gary Mason was. And their parents would have to tilt their heads and ponder for a moment before it suddenly hit them. "Wasn't he the guy who was writing a book?"

The second and third periods that night went smoothly, even

if I didn't get a goal. Every time I looked up and fired a pass to Marcel Dionne, I still had a hard time believing it. There were a couple of times when we were moving the puck pretty good and had the other team on the run, and I was dishing the puck back to the defence and the defence was dishing it back to me and then I'd find someone open in the slot, and the puck would be in the net a second later. The crowd loved it, and for one night at least I could pretend I had always been one of these guys.

There was a particularly enthusiastic group at the post-game reception. It had been a good and appreciative crowd; they were true fans of the players.

After the players had gobbled on chicken wings and washed them down with a few beers, people were lined up in front of them for autographs. One of them was Denis Savoie, the thirty-nine-year-old owner of a local takeout restaurant called To Gos. Savoie was originally from New Brunswick and heard there was work in Inuvik because of oil and gas exploration, so he decided to check it out. He was a huge hockey fan, just as his father was.

Denis Savoie had eighty hockey jerseys in his basement, he told me. And every Saturday night he watched hockey, just as he did with his father growing up. He couldn't believe some of the players he got to watch this night. Russ Courtnall was always one of his hockey pool picks. It seemed like it was only yesterday when he saw Bob Rouse take his turn holding the Stanley Cup aloft.

"Why do you think people still care for old NHL players?" I asked Savoie.

"Because we know them," said Savoie. "They represent a time in the game when we knew the players. We could see them. Lafleur, Dionne, Orr, Hull, Bower, these people were gods when I was growing up. That's not the case anymore, for a whole bunch of reasons. People resent the money the guys make now, and there isn't that connection with the fans that there once was.

"I mean, nowadays you don't even know half the players in the league. It has been so watered down. A lot of the players are just nameless people who will be out of the league in a few years. There aren't the Lafleurs and the Dionnes and the Hulls and the Orrs anymore, are there? And I don't think there will be. I think a lot of people have such good memories of these guys—that's why we come out to these kinds of games. It's a way to say thanks. Tonight, I wish my dad had been able to see Dionne with me. He would have loved that."

This is what I heard on this trip. From the Denis Savoies. From everyone. The NHL Oldtimers represented good memories. For most people at the games, the players took them back to their childhoods, with their parents, in a living room somewhere in Canada. That's why they were so happy to see Johnny Bower. He was like an old friend they hadn't seen in years. Now here he was in person. This was their opportunity to say, "Thanks for the memories." These weren't has-beens on the ice. Their skills could never be diminished, at least not in the eyes of those watching.

After the banquet, we piled into the vans and headed back to the Eskimo Inn. A group of us, the usual suspects—Nylund, Courtnall, Rouse, Bodger, Lofthouse—headed out on the town, such as it was, for a few beers. The first place we visited was called The Zoo, where fist fights and knife fights weren't uncommon. Our group was pretty quickly identified as being former NHLers, and free beers arrived at our table almost as soon as we sat down.

But the general atmosphere was chilly to hostile.

"You guys get free beer?" someone at a nearby table said out loud. "What a joke that is. With all the money you make, and you get free drinks on top of that."

We tried to keep to ourselves. Someone came over to get Russ Courtnall's autograph and asked if he could get a picture with him. No problem, Russ said. We weren't long for The Zoo, however, and decided to try The Mad Trapper, since it was right across from our hotel and we could quickly retreat to our rooms if the atmosphere wasn't better than The Zoo's. A couple of the guys bailed. We found a table near the back, and soon people were approaching for autographs and pictures.

"Which one of you is Tiger Williams?" one middle-aged woman asked.

Doug Bodger pointed to me.

"You're Tiger?" she asked.

I decided to go along with it.

"Yeah, I'm Tiger, waddaya want?" I said in the best, gravelly voiced impression of Williams that I could muster.

"A picture."

She moved around and put her arm around me while a friend with a camera set up in front of us. Snap. Then she asked for an autograph.

"You're a real pain in the ass," I said. I signed a napkin.

"Okay. There you go. Now get the hell out of here."

The guys were laughing. I figured I hadn't said anything that Tiger wouldn't have said anyway.

After a quick beer, we'd seen enough. Outside it had to be minus thirty. It wouldn't take long, we figured, to freeze to death. The sky was brilliant and filled with stars. The Arctic Ocean wasn't that far away. We ran across the street, into the warm lobby of the Eskimo Inn. Tomorrow we were off to Alaska.

CHAPTER 5

A NIGHT AT THE DOG SLED SALOON

I SETTLED INTO a seat next to Paul Reinhart for the two-hour flight from Inuvik to Fairbanks as the tour moved into Alaska.

Reinhart was one of those people whose off-ice personality mirrored the player he was while on it. He seemed to glide through life on a thick cushion of self-confidence. He was also a true gentleman who made you feel that anything you had to say was important. When you spoke, you could tell he was listening because of the questions he asked. He exuded smarts, and it was no surprise to learn he had done well financially after hanging up his skates.

On the ice, Reinhart was as smooth as a thousand-year-old pebble. In the rough-and-tumble world of the National Hockey League, he stood out for the intelligent way in which he played the game. Although he was as competitive as the next person, Reinhart believed in playing fair, not dirty, and that gratuitous violence, like spearing and butt-ending, cheapened the game.

Reinhart was in a talkative mood. He had views and thoughts on just about everything and was delighted to look back on his career, which began in Atlanta. He had been the Flames' first pick in the 1979 entry draft, twelfth overall, a silky-smooth-skating defenceman from the Kitchener Rangers of the Ontario Hockey League. Far from being upset about being picked by a team universally regarded as lousy, Reinhart saw it as a challenge. And he saw himself as part of a larger plan to turn the club around.

Reinhart wasn't expected to make the team in his first year, but after an exceptionally strong training camp, coaches had no choice but to give him a spot. Reinhart loved everything about that first year in Atlanta. His teammates. The coaching staff. Even the fans who didn't know a whole lot about the game. And when word broke that the team would be leaving and relocating to Calgary, there was an initial period of shock.

"A lot of us didn't want to go," Reinhart remembered. "We even talked about throwing in money to see if we could save the team. But it was a done deal, and pretty soon we all woke up in Calgary."

Playing to raucous crowds at the 6,500-seat Stampede Corral rink, the new Calgary Flames instantly became the hottest ticket in town. The team had a legitimate star in Kent Nilsson, a supremely talented Swedish forward, while Pat Riggin had established himself as a standout in net. That first season, the Flames made a surprise run in the playoffs, beating out Chicago and Philadelphia before finally falling to Minnesota in the semifinals. It was enough, though, to make Reinhart and his teammates the darlings of the city. "They even had a parade for us, just for making it to the semifinals," Reinhart recalled.

Most of all, however, he remembered the birth of the Battle of Alberta.

"That first year, the 1980–81 season, the Oilers were knocked out in the first round by Montreal," Reinhart recalled. "When we beat out Philly, I remember about five or six of the Oiler players coming down to Calgary to congratulate us and offer support the rest of the way. That summer we did some charity events together and golfed with some of the guys, and it was all very collegial.

"The following year, though, it got real competitive. The Oilers felt they were a team on the rise, and they knew they'd have to always get past us to go anywhere. And all of a sudden the games between the two teams were vicious. I mean they were just ugly, ugly games. Every year you looked at the calendar to see when we played them. A certain side of you dreaded the games, and another side looked forward to them. But boy, the stuff that went on! There was spearing, slashing, slew-footing, sucker-punches, two guys fighting one guy. As good as the hockey was, it could have been so much better had there not been so much crap going on. But you knew that every game, four or five guys on each team were going to fight.

"In the dressing room our guys used to plan the fights. It was almost like they were choreographed. Tim Hunter would kind of diagram it out, and Jim Peplinski and a couple of the other guys would be listening and it was like, 'Okay, when the puck drops, I'll grab so-and-so. When that happens, this guy will probably try to move in. You grab him. Then you go and grab that other guy.' It was amazing. And sure enough, the puck would drop and it would all unfold just the way Hunter described it."

For a few of those years in Calgary, Reinhart played for Bob Johnson, the legendary coach whose favourite expression, "It's a great day for hockey," became a fitting epithet upon his death in 1991. Johnson had come out of the U.S. College hockey system and had some things to learn about the game at the NHL level. He was a thinking-person's coach, therefore one who Reinhart could relate to better than others.

Reinhart also had some sympathy for his coach, a gentle soul who in some ways seemed out of his element in the often crude world of the NHL locker room. Some players, Reinhart recalled, would often do or say something gross in front of Johnson just to get a reaction. But usually Johnson didn't bat an eye. "I remember guys used to walk into his office completely nude just to see what he'd say, and he wouldn't even acknowledge it. He was great."

As Reinhart looked back on his career, he felt fortunate. He got to play some old-time NHL hockey alongside some of the true legends of the game. But he was also able to hang around long enough to cash in on the dramatic increase in salaries that began to take effect in the late 1980s. "I was lucky," Reinhart said that morning above the din of the plane's engines. "The oldtimers didn't make the money, and a lot of the guys today will never have the opportunity to play old-time hockey. That's where I lucked out. I mean, I played with Davie Keon and Gordie Howe. I know they weren't in their primes, but they were still legends of the game. I played against Wayne Cashman and Terry O'Reilly, but I also played against Gretzky and Messier. I am much more grateful for that fact looking back than I was at the time."

Which brought Reinhart, in his always eloquent and insightful way, to the trip we were on. More specifically, to why many of the guys, the younger ones especially, would leave the comfort of their expensive hockey-built homes to lug their equipment around for meal money. Russ Courtnall wasn't an Oldtimer in the sense the public imagined. Nor was Gary Nylund or Doug Bodger or Bob Rouse. Some of them had been out of the NHL for only a year or two. So why were they here? Were they that desperate for a road trip again? Reinhart figured it was because they all started playing long enough ago that they still appreciated tradition and what guys like Tiger Williams and Marcel Dionne and Johnny Bower did for the game before they came along. And some of them had been taken under the wings of the real Oldtimers when they first entered the NHL.

But Reinhart wondered about the players of today. The ones just entering the league. Who among them had that same sense of tradition? Who was going to bridge the Johnny Bowers to the Marcel Dionnes to the Wayne Gretzkys?

"I was that bridge when I played. It was my generation, therefore, that I think was the most fortunate in that we played with Original Six guys and we made some money too. Not what they're making today, mind you. At the end of the day most people would probably say they'd take the money, and we can't argue with that or fight them on it but boy, they have no appreciation of the past. That's why these Oldtimers tours will be among the last. The guys playing hockey today won't go on tours like this because they won't feel the need to. They sure won't have to do it for the money, the way others do.

"The guys today don't have that link to the great players whose lives weren't materially affected because of the riches they got from their abilities as hockey players. So the guys today don't have any sense of Johnny Bower playing twenty-five years in professional hockey (ten in the minors) but only becoming an NHLer at thirty-six and winning a Stanley Cup at forty-two. They have no appreciation for a guy who was making $13,000 a year, had won a Stanley Cup, a Vézina, a Conn Smythe, wanted a hefty raise and was told he would take $2,500 or go back to the minors."

Today's NHL player wasn't the only thing that had changed in recent years. The relationship between the fan and the athletes had changed too. And it mostly had to do with the perception that professional athletes today, regardless of the sport, were mostly a bunch of overpaid, spoiled brats.

"In the stands, money is all you hear people talk about," Reinhart said. "What you hear is, so and so isn't working very hard and that son of a bitch is going to make more this year than I'll make in my lifetime. That's the perception. The reality is that guy is working hard, probably a lot harder than a lot of old-time hockey players did. Significantly harder. But the perception is, because the old guys didn't make much money they played for the love of the game.

"The reality is the guys today are far better players, far superior athletes, are in much better condition and work significantly harder and bring more to their game every night because they have far more to lose."

That morning, as our plane sailed through a bright northern sky, Reinhart mourned the loss of characters from the game as well. It was almost like today's players were produced by cookie cutters, so similar were they in the way they skated, shot the puck, built up their bodies. And in the way they acted, too: most coached from an early age on what to say before and after games and how to avoid unwanted attention. Reinhart felt it all had to do with the enormity of what was at stake for today's players— the money, the fame, the endorsement opportunities.

The public was sick of the seemingly daily off-field, off-ice incidents involving today's athletes, and the media, of course, were always ready to pounce on the slightest indiscretion.

"In my era and Johnny Bower's era before that, there were lots of guys pulled over for drinking and driving," Reinhart recalled. "Today that makes huge headlines everywhere. Look at Teemu Selanne or Sergei Fedorov. In my day it was like, 'Hey, you crazy nut, nudge, nudge, wink, wink.'

"You talk about role models—the public today is weary about athletes as role models because of things you hear and the image today's athletes have. Back in the old days, the public was prepared to turn a blind eye to the antics of hockey players and how they prepared themselves for games and what they did after the game was over. They were perceived to be role models, and yet they were probably far from the ideal role model. Today's athletes are probably much better suited to be role models. They're in better shape, they don't party as much. They're much more professionally prepared. They take care of themselves, and yet the perception is they're spoiled, they're lazy, they're not good role models. And most of that is linked to the money they make. It's interesting."

Reinhart played in the NHL for eleven seasons. His best year was 1982–83, when he racked up 75 points on 17 goals and 58 assists. During the 1989 entry draft, he and Steve Bozek were traded to the Vancouver Canucks for a third-round draft choice. He was ready to begin a new phase in his career but was dogged by a nagging injury.

Reinhart had injured his back while weightlifting six years earlier. It would never be the same again, thanks, in part, to some shoddy treatment at the time. Even today, years after his last game, there are good days and bad days.

"I'm not disappointed with my career," said Reinhart. "I played more than four hundred games. But I am very, very disappointed that I ended up with the back I did. I still have my episodes. If it had not been for the back, given the way I played the game, I would have played until I was forty. I was even told that."

Reinhart came from a family of accountants. So when some investment opportunities came his way while he was in Calgary, he did what came naturally to him; he studied the proposals in excruciating detail and then made a decision. He got involved with some early-stage mineral exploration companies that had some success. Reinhart would have enough wins and capital late in his hockey career that he would be able to carry on and make more investments.

"It ultimately made the transition from hockey to the real world much easier," said Reinhart, who today looks just as comfortable in a pinstripe suit as in hockey pants and a jersey. "I was fortunate to be involved in some good companies and get hooked up with some good people. Venture capital isn't for everybody, but some early-stage investing is ideal for young guys with earning power and cash flow. Hockey was a great cash flow business because every two weeks you got your cheque. What was going on in the economy wasn't affecting our paycheque. So we had the opportunity to become good shareholders in companies because we could buy and we could hold on for a long time, and sometimes it worked out extremely well."

Reinhart was already well-off financially before he retired as a Canuck. But it was in Vancouver that the hockey player formed a friendship with Ross Davidson, then the team's orthopedic surgeon, who was looking for some investment opportunities of his own. "Davidson knew some guys who were starting up a bio-tech company," said Reinhart modestly. "We helped raise them some money and invested ourselves, and it happened to become a huge Canadian and North American success story."

Angiotech, which produced a type of anti-cancer drug, went from a startup in 1994 to a billion-dollar company today. Stock went from twenty-five cents to as high as $130 at one point. In the process, Reinhart became a prosperous man. Always on the lookout for another opportunity, he took a major position in a professional lacrosse team in Vancouver in 2001 and was poised to invest even more in what he called "second-tier" sports franchises.

"I think there is a way to make money in sports when you are providing entertainment in an affordable way to people who otherwise can't get to these events. If you can make money in a business venture on the backs of butts in the seats, if you can sell tickets and cover your overhead and pay your players and make some money with just your crowd, I think there is an avenue for that in the sports world."

With his track record, who was going to argue with him?

We had talked nearly the whole way to Fairbanks and now the plane was landing. It was the first trip to Alaska for many of us.

AFTER COLLECTING our suitcases and equipment we hopped on a bus that took us to our hotel, the famous Captain Bartlett Inn. If it wasn't famous before we arrived, it would be by the time we left.

The Bartlett was built in 1975 to house pipeline workers working in Fairbanks. It had been named in honour of Captain Robert Bartlett, who, according to hotel lore, was the greatest ice navigator of the last century. Born in Newfoundland in 1875, Bartlett had spent more than fifty years mapping the waters of the far north and leading over twenty expeditions to the Arctic. The name of the hotel was apparently a long-overdue tribute to a seaman one presumed was a long-lost descendant of whoever owned the place.

The Bartlett looked like a turn-of-the-century lodge, built with spruce logs. The main lobby looked like a taxidermy museum; it had stuffed muskox, Alaskan brown bear, rams, deer, wolves, foxes, you name it, on display. The hardwood floor was covered with an autumn-themed carpet, a mosaic of greens and oranges and yellows with falling leaves frozen in flight. Off the main lobby was the dining room, the Musher's Roadhouse. Next to the dining room was the room we really cared about—the Dog Sled Saloon.

The Musher's Roadhouse and the Dog Sled Saloon were named in honour of the Yukon Quest, the most demanding dog sled race in the world. The Captain Bartlett Inn often sponsored a team in the race. Inside the Dog Sled were bibs worn by Quest racers over the years as well as other bits of memorabilia, including an actual dog sled. American dollar bills were placed under the glass tops of the tables patrons drank at, an idea someone had come up with years ago. But the best part of the Dog Sled was the peanuts that customers were given to munch on. Patrons could toss their peanut shells on the floor, which only added to the Dog Sled's unique charm.

The game was being played at the Big Dipper Arena, a wonderfully quirky rink that had mirrored tiles on the ceiling. No one was quite sure why this was so, but we tried to imagine how weird it would be to be knocked flat on your ass during a game only to look up and see yourself sprawled out on the ice.

Fairbanks had put together a team of local firefighters that included a few ringers. And soon after the puck was dropped that night, it was evident that the string of late nights was catching up to a few of the guys. In the first period, Wayne Babych was having a heck of a time staying on his feet. He'd get knocked off the puck, struggle to get back up, get knocked off the puck again. One time he tried to get back on his feet and looked like a baby deer trying to get to its feet for the first time. On the bench, the guys were killing themselves laughing. Unlike most of the games on the schedule, which began at seven in the evening, the Fairbanks tussle started at two in the afternoon. Maybe that accounted for some of the lethargy.

Richard Brodeur, who wasn't used to many shots in these games, was getting plenty of action and looked very much like the King Richard of the Canucks' run to the Stanley Cup finals in 1982. For someone who had just turned fifty-one and who had battled weight problems, Brodeur was surprisingly agile and quick. By the end of the period, the NHLers had gone up 3–1, but not with any ease.

At each stop, local organizers had a couple of local minor hockey players hang around the Oldtimers bench in the event that one of the players needed something. "What I need," Bob Rouse told one of the kids, "is a bucket of steam." The boy looked puzzled. "Where would I get it?" he asked. Rouse suggested that the kid and his friend try and get it from a hot dog machine or a kettle. "I really need it."

The kids took off, determined to get a bucket of steam.

Rouse returned to the bench from a shift early in the second period of the game to find that the two kids had returned. One was holding a styrofoam cup filled with coffee. "This is all we could find," said the one boy. "I asked at the concession and no one could figure out how to keep the steam in a bucket. This is all they could come up with."

Rouse feigned disappointment.

"Well, we can try this, but I'm not sure it's going to work."

Rouse grabbed the cup and began carefully lifting the lid. Then he grabbed the blade of his hockey stick and brought it up near the top of the cup, as if he needed the steam to do some work on his stick. The little bit of steam that was in the cup quickly escaped. "Darn," he said, apparently exasperated. "Do you think there's any left?"

The boys looked inside the cup.

"Don't think so."

"Well, you're going to have to go and get some more," said Rouse. "And see if you can get a stick lengthener, too."

"What's that?"

"You've never seen a stick lengthener before?"

"No."

"You use it to stretch the length of your stick."

The kids took off again, this time in search of a "stick lengthener," which, of course, didn't exist except in the playfully cruel mind of Bob Rouse.

After a scare in the opening twenty minutes, the Oldtimers found their legs. Well, Babych found his at least, and then began potting one goal after another. Courtnall was flying, and Nylund was joining the rush. And there were smiles once again on the Oldtimers bench.

"Hey, mister."

Rouse turned to see his two buddies standing by the bench, empty-handed.

"What happened?"

"We asked everyone and no one knew what a stick lengthener was. We must have asked twenty people, and no one ever heard of it."

Rouse gave the kids a couple of pucks and thanked them for trying. He would have to wait until the next town to get his steam and stick lengthener, he said.

When the final horn sounded to end the game, the Fairbanks crowd stood and gave both teams a loud and sustained ovation. The Oldtimers didn't know what to expect in Fairbanks and were pleased with how enthusiastic the fans were. The post-game reception was back at the Captain Bartlett Inn. I decided to catch an hour's sleep instead of dinner. When I woke up and headed down to the banquet a couple of hours later, most of the locals were gone but the party was just getting going.

Doug Bodger had joined a violin player named Earl Hughes at the front of the room. Suddenly it was karaoke time, and The Bodge had a full head of steam. It was hard to make out all the words but the song had something to do with a rising sun, we were all sure of that. One song led to another. When he finally wrapped up, Bodge had the audience eating out of his hand. The twenty-two-ounce beers being served might have had something to do with it, as well as the endless stream of house wine that kept arriving, but for a former NHL defenceman he was pretty good.

Russ Courtnall told the story of the time he and Bodger ended up in a hotel bar where a guy was toiling on a piano and no one appeared remotely interested in his songs. After a few beers, Bodger got up the nerve to wander over to the piano. He asked if the musician knew "Piano Man," by Billy Joel. Before any-one knew it, Bodger was belting out "Piano Man" like the original artist.

"The piano player had this tip jar on the piano that was empty," Courtnall remembered of the evening. "Well, after two or three songs, people started wandering over to the piano and started joining in. Then a few more people arrive, and the guy's tip jar starts going up and up and up. It was hilarious. And after every song the guy would look at Bodge and say, 'What would you like to hear now?'"

Bodger was not the only entertainer in the bunch. When he played in Chicago with the Blackhawks, Gary Nylund had joined a band that included members of the NFL Chicago Bears and the MLB Cubs. He got to learn his way around a guitar, even though he'd never taken a lesson in his life. Now he was going solo and performing a collection of his hits, starting with the theme song to *Gilligan's Island.*

I can't recall what the other songs were, but I do know they were greeted with thunderous applause, the kind usually reserved for a Bruce Springsteen encore. We were now starting to receive noise complaints from other sections of the restaurant, so we shut down the music and headed to the Dog Sled Saloon, which was right next door.

Everyone was in fine form by this point. Tiger was always in the middle of some story and seemed to be a one-man tourist attraction everywhere he went. Every so often he would do something to get people's attention, one time by whipping an empty beer glass at Bodger for the fun of it. If it was intended for Bodger's head it was a poor shot, as it ended up hitting the former Sabres defenceman square in the ass. Tiger could get wild after consuming a few. I recalled one story he told about a banquet he was at in Vancouver. For most of the evening, he had been pestered by some guy who didn't like Tiger Williams and decided to let him know it. After warning the guy several times to back off and get out of his face, Williams decided to take matters into his owns hands.

He grabbed a fork.

Williams poked the guy right in the cheek with it.

"You could see the four little marks in his face from the fork," Williams said. "He never bothered me after that."

Bob Rouse was standing at a nearby table with some of the guys. Rouse was an interesting study. If you didn't know him well you would think he was a fairly serious sort, almost humourless. In reality he was one of the funniest people alive, especially if you liked your wit particularly dry.

He was always at the end of some gag, like the ones where he was sending some poor kid off to get a bucket of steam or a stick lengthener. On one of the flights, Rouse got some shaving cream and reprised Jimmy Mann's famous stunt on John Ferguson. In Rouse's case, the victim wasn't anyone nearly as volatile or potentially violent as Ferguson. Instead, it was a young kid in his early twenties who served as the main auctioneer of NHL memorabilia at the various post-game receptions.

The poor kid was fast asleep when Rouse struck. And a fine job it was, the cream swirled atop the young man's shiny black hair like an ice cream cone from Dairy Queen. Once it was applied, it was just a matter of waiting for the victim to wake up. He did, eventually, just minutes before we were to touch down. No one said a word. Not even his young partner, who was also asleep at the time of the attack and had woken to see what had happened, but who also knew it was probably not a good idea to say anything.

It was a perfectly stupid, childish prank. We all knew that. But for some reason, twenty thousand feet in the air, among a tired and giddy group of hockey players, it seemed hilarious. Every time I looked at the kid, who was now awake and talking to others on the plane, I had to bite down hard on my lip to stop from bursting out laughing. And when he started talking to me, it wasn't easy to keep my eyes from drifting upward towards the top of his head, which would have tipped him off that something was, ah, up, so to speak.

Eventually the kid ended up touching his head for some reason and discovered that there was something on it besides the gel he had applied that morning. In the seat behind him, Rouse sat expressionless as the kid looked around for the likely prankster.

Rouse was one of those people the hockey gods had simply chosen to smile upon. He was never the best defenceman on any of the teams he played for, even going back to minor hockey. He wasn't good enough to make a rep team for years. But eventually he did, and every year he got a bit better and eventually did enough things right to take his talents to the NHL.

He was originally drafted by the Minnesota North Stars, eightieth overall, in the 1982 entry draft. He played in Minnesota for the better part of five seasons before being traded to Washington. He hung around there for a few more seasons before the Capitals ended up moving him and Peter Zezel in January 1991 to Toronto, in exchange for Al Iafrate.

During his three and a half seasons with the Leafs, the team transformed itself from an annual disappointment and national joke into a playoff contender. Two of the years in which Rouse was in a Leafs uniform, the team went to the Western Conference finals, losing both times.

In the summer of 1994, Rouse became a Group 5 free agent, the first to move through the system. Under the collective bargaining agreement between the NHL and its players union, anyone who had played in the league for ten years and was still making below the league average was eligible for free agency. Rouse fit the bill.

Never flashy but always solid, Rouse had developed into one of those defenceman that teams aspiring to the Stanley Cup always wanted in their lineup. He rarely made mistakes. He was tough in front of his own net. He was a great team guy who could add some veteran leadership in the dressing room. He had blossomed into the kind of player that Scotty Bowman, coach of the Detroit Red Wings, felt might be one of the final key pieces of the Stanley Cup puzzle in Hockeytown.

And he was right.

"What were those Cup years in Detroit like?" I asked Rouse as we stood around a table sipping a couple of beers.

What Rouse had to say surprised me a little bit. I had covered both of Detroit's Stanley Cup wins in 1996–97 and 1997–98. While I hadn't covered the team on a daily basis, Detroit appeared to be as tight a team as you could find. According to Rouse, however, there was certainly enough friction along the way to have derailed their Stanley Cup dreams.

"Steve Yzerman was a good leader, but he needed support," said Rouse. "I was good at bringing that support together. If Stevie said something and you could see a couple of guys rolling their eyes, that's where I would step in. If you saw any kind of dissension, you tried to nip it in the bud.

"There was a bit of a rift between Sergei Fedorov and Yzerman. You just had to get in their heads a little bit and say, 'Stevie, you need Sergei playing his best for us to be successful,' and vice versa."

Part of the problem stemmed from a perception by many North American players in the NHL that the Russians had a me-first, money-first attitude. The Wings had plenty of Russians back then, a group that included Fedorov, Igor Larionov, Vladimir Konstantinov, Victor Koslov and Viacheslav Fetisov, so the potential for trouble was real. "When you saw that attitude, you might have some Canadian and U.S. players saying 'What the hell is this guy doing?' And you have to find a way to smooth that over. You have to say, 'Hey, he has his motivation for playing; you have yours. It's going to work in everyone's best interests if you get along with this guy.' That's what I was doing a lot of in Detroit. Trying to keep things smoothed over."

The year before Detroit's Cup win in 1996–97, the Wings thought they had the team to take it all. The Wings had won first place overall that year in the NHL, plowing through the opposition with such ease that the team became instant favourites to go all the way. The coaches, meantime, were worried that the regular season had been such a breeze the Wings wouldn't be ready for the second season—the post-season. The playoffs were always tougher and took more out of teams. And if you weren't hungry, you could easily get eaten yourself.

Which is precisely what happened to Detroit that year, as they ended up losing to Colorado in the Western Conference finals. Colorado would go on to win the Cup that year.

The next season, Rouse recalled that night in the Dog Sled Saloon, the Red Wings coaches would be mindful of the lessons learned the previous year.

"I remember talking to the assistant coaches, and they were trying to lose games, if you can imagine that," Rouse recalled. "Like, they would take some of our better players out of the lineup or not play them as much, trying to get the guys to just lose some games and break things up because they didn't want to go into the playoffs completely dominating like that again. They wanted to make sure we weren't vulnerable like we had been a season earlier."

When the Wings won the Cup, it was everything Rouse thought it would be. The Wings had done it in devastating fashion, too, disposing of the troubled Philadelphia Flyers in four games straight. Best of all, the Wings were able to finish the series off in front of their hometown fans.

"It was an amazing feeling that night," Rouse remembered of the Wings' first Cup win in forty-two years. "The building was so loud for that final game. In the dressing room later, it was just insane. The champagne, the media, it was just crazy."

And then, less than a week later, all of the celebration would come crashing to an end.

"We had a team function at this golf course," Rouse began. "It was called Orchard Grove or Orchard Park. It was going to be a great day. We had the Cup out on the course with us. A lot of the guys took limos, including the Russians, because we knew there was going to be some drinking. We had a few skins games going on. It was just a real innocent fun time.

"The Russian guys left a little early. It wasn't that much longer after they took off that someone got a call on their cell phone that one of the limos had been in an accident. The first impression was it was no big deal. Like it was probably a fender-bender of some kind. But a few calls later and it's, like, everyone is in the hospital and one person's dead. That turned out to be a false report, but that was how serious the accident was."

As it turned out, the limo was being driven that June 13 night by Richard Gnida, a chauffeur with a history of drug and alcohol problems. Blood tests later showed traces of marijuana in his system. There were three Red Wings in the limo when Gnida drove the car onto a median and into a tree: Fetisov, Konstantinov and the team masseur, Sergei Mnatsakanov. The injuries to Fetisov would be much less serious than the ones suffered by the other two. (Gnida was not seriously hurt.)

"After hearing that the guys were in the hospital, we all headed up there," Rouse continued. "By the time we got there, it was complete panic. Myself and Nick Lidstrom, I think it was, ended up going into the room where Vlady was being kept, and he was hooked up to everything imaginable. It was just awful. It made you feel sick because you could tell how serious it was. But after a while we were told there was nothing we could do, so we all went home and listened to the news for developments."

It ruined what should have been a particularly special Stanley Cup summer. Every day, it seemed, more news would trickle out about the accident and the condition of Konstantinov and Mnatsakanov. The news about their condition just seemed to get worse. When it was Rouse's turn to get the Cup for a few days, much of the joy was lost. "You felt bad for celebrating," he remembered.

The following season, the accident became a rallying cry for the Wings. "Do it for Vlady!" the players were reminded, seemingly every day.

Although it was a noble cause, it sometimes became a little much for players like Rouse. The next year, perhaps because they were drawing inspiration from their fallen comrades or just because they were a dominant hockey team, the Wings would reprise their Stanley Cup victory, beating the Washington Capitals four games straight. When the final siren sounded, Konstantinov was wheeled onto the ice in his Red Wings sweater and handed the Cup in one of the most memorable Cup scenes ever.

That would be the end of Rouse's run with the Wings. The following season he would sign with San Jose. The combination of his new contract with the Sharks and the deal he had signed with Detroit provided Rouse with almost as much cash in his last five years in the NHL as he had made in the previous twelve. He made millions. Certainly enough that money wouldn't be an issue after retirement. And enough to allow him to leave the game on his terms. "I didn't want to spend another year living in hotels on the road," Rouse said as another round of beers arrived. "I had a good career. Had a couple of Cups now. You know, there's a lot you miss out on playing hockey. My kids were getting older, and I'd never gone out trick-or-treating with them. It's probably one of my favourite holidays because it's such a senseless thing. You dress up and knock on doors for candy."

Rouse laughed. "I missed that. I missed going to their games. Now I finally have a chance to do that. Even in the summers, when I was playing, our friends would be going boating or doing this or that and I'd have to take a pass to work out. After a while you start to resent hockey a bit. When you're playing they don't give you an itinerary until the day before you're leaving on a trip. You can't plan anything. You're thirty-something years old and you have a curfew—even though I never missed one. Just the fact that someone is telling you you have to be in at ten o'clock, it just pisses you off after a while."

But, like any of his teammates on the Oldtimers tour, Rouse wouldn't have traded it for anything. He'd met so many great people, been to so many great places. For a kid growing up in Surrey, B.C., who couldn't even make his local rep team, Bob Rouse hadn't done too badly. He would finish with 1,031 games in the top hockey league in the world and become the 133rd NHL player to play one thousand games.

"That's a pretty good achievement," Rouse said, sounding as serious as he would ever be on this trip.

I looked at my watch. It said 2:30 A.M. The Dog Sled was still packed. Doug Bodger was starting to sing. I knew it was time for bed.

CHAPTER 6

SCORING IN KENAI

IT WAS QUIET on the plane. As quiet as it had been on any flight of the trip.

The night before had taken its toll. There were varying reports on when things had finally shut down at the Dog Sled. Tiger remembered crawling to bed around five thirty in the morning. A few others had packed it in just ahead of him. In general, the team was in pain, and if there had been a day off built into the itinerary, this is when the Oldtimers could have used it.

There wasn't much interest in staring out the window, even though it was a glorious day, one in which the land below seemed to stretch forever. Most of the players turned their jackets or sweaters into pillows and drifted off before the plane's tires had left the ground. It was a short flight, just over an hour. Everyone started to wake up as we started our descent into Kenai, and the outline of hundreds of small lakes and rivers and streams, covered in snow, came into view. It must look stunning in the summertime, when the area is invaded by thousands of tourists ready to test Kenai's claim as the King Salmon Capital of the World.

After landing we strolled into the small airport, which looked as if it had been decorated by the local taxidermist. Mounted fish and stuffed grizzlies, brown bears and wolverines greeted us. This was the north, the display screamed, an area to be enjoyed but also respected. Our group had congregated around a stuffed brown bear standing on its haunches. It had to be ten feet tall, and each of its claws was longer than a finger. "These are mean, mean animals," a local who had come to pick us up said. "They can shred a moose in minutes. They eat people, animals, anything they can get their hands on. This is not Disneyland, folks. This is one mean animal that is not be to messed with. This isn't the movies up here. This is real life."

A few of us looked at each another, trying hard not to roll our eyes. The impromptu dissertation on the brown bear sounded like a finger-wagging lecture. It was as if we were a bunch of city slickers who assumed you could feed bread crumbs to the bears up here. We knew this wasn't Disneyland and we weren't the Mighty Ducks, although a movie about our adventures didn't seem so far-fetched.

We all piled into a couple of vans and set off for a local pub to have lunch. After the game that night, the plan called for us to head back to the airport and take a quick, twenty-minute flight to Anchorage, where we were scheduled to play the next day. But this meant there was going to be some time to put in between lunch in Kenai and five o'clock, when we would head to the local rink to play our game.

We pulled up to a local sports bar that had a big satellite dish on the roof. Inside, hockey sweaters were hung on the walls with posters of some of today's NHL players. There were TVs everywhere, some turned to a premier league soccer game, others to American football. A few of us grabbed a table and ordered a beer, figuring a little "hair of the dog" might make us feel better.

"What day is it?" asked Johnny Bower.

"Sunday, John," someone blurted out.

"Sunday, yeah, I thought it was."

Johnny smiled, which made us all smile. It was wonderful having Johnny around. He was a warm, grandfatherly person, who had a million stories to tell but seldom shared them because he was either shy or modest or didn't think anyone would be interested. He seldom opened up, but when he did, everyone would go quiet and the floor would be turned over without any resistance. And then he would tell a story about his days with the Leafs, or about Punch Imlach, and then he'd laugh and that would be it. He wasn't the least bit interested, it seemed, in reliving his glory days. He didn't want to be like an old soldier talking about battles he fought, about friends who were dead. He seemed self-conscious when only he was talking and everyone else was listening. Sometimes you had to draw the stories out of him.

"Where did you get that stitch from?" someone asked Johnny, pointing to an inch-long scar that sat on top of his eyebrow.

"Oh, I got that after we won the Stanley Cup in '64," Johnny replied. "I threw my stick so far up in the air when the game was over I forgot about it. Well, it came crashing down right on my face. I think it was six or seven stitches to close it."

Actually, Bower's face didn't look too bad for someone who had played twenty-five years without a face mask. He had tried one near the end of his career but hated it. He felt it restricted his vision. By then, however, the main thing hurting his sight was age. In his final year, 1970, Bower played one game for the Leafs and then decided to hang up the pads for good. He was forty-four years old. Bower once estimated that he took 250 stitches to his face alone during his career. Whenever a puck caused swelling over the eye, the Leafs trainer used to put a leech on it. The leech would latch itself onto the bump and gorge itself until it virtually exploded. By then the swelling was down and Bower was able to return to the game.

Earlier in the trip, Bower had regaled Paul Reinhart and some of the others with a story about the time he went looking for a raise from the Leafs' coach and GM, Punch Imlach. The Leafs were coming off a Stanley Cup win in 1964, and Bower was complaining to his teammate George Armstrong that he deserved a raise. Armstrong couldn't believe that Bower was making only thirteen thousand dollars, given everything he meant to the team, and encouraged his goalie to demand a ten-thousand-dollar raise.

By all accounts, however, Bower was as meek and mild back in his playing days as he was in retirement, coaching the NHL Oldtimers. He was certainly no match for Imlach, who was everything Bower was not—stubborn, vociferous, mean, rude, bullying. The first time Bower asked Imlach for a meeting to discuss a raise, Imlach told him to get out of his office and that if he was one minute late for practice he'd be fined fifty dollars. Eventually, Bower got King Clancy on his side, who helped the quiet goaltender get a $2,500 raise.

After retiring in 1970, Bower moved into scouting for the Leafs and then became the team's goaltending coach. But Bower was far from a rich man, which is partially why he was on this tour. Yes, meeting old fans was wonderful and being around the guys made him feel young, but Bower spent hours and hours of his time up in his room, signing pictures of himself that were sold at each stop. He would get five dollars or so for each autographed picture, and if two hundred were sold, that was a thousand dollars. He also got a cut of the autographed Leafs jerseys with his name and number on them, as well the more elaborately framed photos of himself from the Leafs' golden era.

"I didn't make a lot of money when I played," Bower said one afternoon on the trip. "That's why I have to spend all afternoon up in my room signing those pictures. Maybe I didn't play my cards as well as I should have when I was playing, but that's the way it goes. Now I need the money."

You could only imagine what Bower, with his credentials, would be making if he were playing in the NHL today. What would four Stanley Cup wins and two Vézinas be worth a season? Five? Six? Seven million a year? And Bower's best season in the late 1960s was probably twenty thousand dollars. It didn't seem right. And yet you didn't get the sense that Johnny Bower felt there had been any great injustice done. That was just the way it was. And he would have been the first to admit that he didn't have the kind of aggressive, abrasive personality you needed to get more money out of team owners back when he played.

After spending the better part of thirteen years riding the buses in the minors before getting his first legitimate shot at the NHL at the age of thirty-four, maybe Bower was just happy to have made it after all those years in the American Hockey League. And maybe, when you're born into a poor family from Prince Albert, Saskatchewan, and you had to use frozen horse droppings as pucks, then you count your blessings when you're getting a regular cheque, regardless of the amount.

Maybe that's what made Bower what he was—likeable, almost sweet. He was the kind of person you wanted to do something for, and yet, it seemed, he was always the one doing the doing, whether it was helping clean up the dressing room, getting pucks on the ice before the game or cheering on a friend.

Paul Reinhart would leave the tour with one unforgettable memory of Bower.

It happened one day when Don Jackson, the former Canadian world figure skating champion who toured with the Oldtimers, was performing his routine between the second and third periods. At the age of sixty-two, Jackson was amazing. He could still do lots of jumps and spins, and he rarely, if ever, took a tumble. His performance to "Singing in the Rain" was quite charming. Still, pulling it all off in front of a few thousand people was never easy.

One game, Reinhart decided to go up on the bench and

watch Jackson's routine, since he'd never seen it. Johnny was up on the bench too.

"He was so sweet," Reinhart remembered of Bower that day. "He knew Don's routine inside out because he'd watched it so much, I guess. And he knew when Don had a big jump coming. And Johnny would be there saying to himself, 'Come on, Donnie, you can do this one, you can do it.' And when Don pulled the jump off, Johnny would punch the air and say, 'Yes.' And then he would do the same thing as Don went into his next jump.

"I couldn't help thinking to myself what a wonderful man Johnny was," Reinhart would recall later. "After everything he's accomplished, here he was, on the bench, rooting Don on. He didn't have to do that. He could have been up signing autographs. But he made it his thing to do. To be there for Don. As much as anything, that says so much about what kind of person Johnny Bower is."

Whenever Johnny had something to say that afternoon in the pub, we all listened. It was like listening to an oral historian. Even if it was a story we'd heard before or read about in some hockey book, it didn't matter. There was nothing like hearing it from someone who was there. It was like he'd stepped right out of the pages of those books and sat down to lunch to tell us himself.

"How good is this?" Bob Rouse said to me as Bower finished telling one of his stories. "Having lunch and listening to Johnny Bower tell stories."

It didn't get any better.

After lunch we still had a few hours to kill before game time. A few locals from Kenai had volunteered their services—and vans—to chauffeur us around. I piled into one with Richard Brodeur, Marcel Dionne, Wayne Babych, Ron Hoggarth and Mark Lofthouse. Ever since we'd touched down in Alaska, we had all talked about seeing an Alaskan moose. And so with time to kill before the game, we set off down the backroads of Kenai looking for Bullwinkle.

About forty-five minutes later, we spotted one in a clearing. It was a mother with her calf, and they were a sight to behold. At first we just got out of the van and stood by the side of the road. But the pair were sixty yards away, and you could barely make them out through the camera lens. So a few of us started wandering up, seeking a better vantage point for pictures but not getting so close that we wouldn't be able to outrun the mother back to the van if she turned on us. We got within twenty-five yards and decided that was close enough. The mother looked up a few times and then went back to grazing and looking for food amid the waist-deep snow.

This was Alaska, we thought.

"There are always a few people around here killed by moose every year," said the local driver who had wandered up with us. "Guy just got killed by one a few weeks ago."

"I've seen enough," said Mark Lofthouse.

"Me too," I chimed in.

Within seconds we were all heading back to the van. It was almost time to head to the arena anyway. I was playing that night and was still desperately looking for my first goal. By the time we reached the rink, Tiger and most of the other players were already there, unpacking their hockey gear from their bags. As usual, Tiger was in fine form and beginning to tell the story about the time he was in Los Angeles, near the end of his career, and he had been kicked out of a game for fighting.

"Our best goalie was Rollie Melanson, and he wasn't playing that night for some reason. I wasn't very happy about it," Williams continued.

"Anyway, I go into the dressing room, and there's Rollie watching the big-screen television we had just got for the room. But he doesn't have it on the game or a sports channel; he was watching some goddamn soap opera. Oh, Christ, was I mad. I just snapped, eh. I went up to the TV and got my stick and smashed it right through the screen. Well, Jesus, the glass went flying everywhere. Rollie took off, he couldn't believe what I just did. But all the glass hit my chest. I didn't have my sweater or shoulder pads on. I had taken it all off. So I head to the shower and there's blood all over the place from the glass hitting me, and I'm trying to get it all off before the game ends and everyone starts piling into the dressing room."

Marcel Dionne, who was a teammate of Williams's at the time, was in the corner of the Oldtimers dressing room howling at the story. And then taking it over.

"I walked into the room and saw the TV and there's the end of a stick, sticking right out of it. I said, 'Jesus Christ, what the hell happened?' And then I see Tiger coming out of the shower and I ask him, 'What the hell happened?' And he pretends like he doesn't know anything. So I go over and take a closer look at the stick. And guess what it says on the shaft? Williams—Number 22. That bastard."

The guys were all laughing. And anytime Williams got that kind of reaction to one of his stories, it usually meant there was another coming right behind it. Tiger's motto seemed to be: why stop when you're on a roll. And he was more than happy to take requests.

"Tell the story about Curt Fraser and the wrestling match," someone suggested.

And Tiger was off.

It seems that one day when Williams and Fraser were teammates in Vancouver with the Canucks, the pair got into a spirited wrestling match shortly after getting out of the shower. Which meant they had no clothes on. As they wrestled, Williams found Fraser's ass staring him right in the face. And so, tiring and looking for a way out of their tussle, Williams shrugged his shoulders and thought, "Why not?"

"I took a huge bite out of his ass," Williams related to the team. "I mean it was *big*. There was blood all over the place. I remember the trainer freaking out, saying one of us could have got infected by doing that. All the guys were laughing, but Curt was pissed because it hurt and he was going to have this big, purple mark on his ass."

And that might have been the end of the story, except for one small thing. Fraser had some explaining to do to his girlfriend. And when he told her the mark was the result of being bitten by Williams in the dressing room, she wasn't having any part of that tale. Biting a teammates' bum was just a little too perverse—even for Tiger. So Fraser was left with no option but to phone his teammate and get him to explain what happened to his girlfriend.

"So he phones me up and asks me to tell her what happened," Williams remembered. "I say, 'Screw off. I'm not telling her.' And I hang up. So he phones back again and asks me again, and I tell him the same thing. And now he's really mad. Finally, later on that night, he phones back a third time and says, 'Thanks a lot, asshole. Now she's gone back to Victoria because she doesn't believe you bit me in the ass.'"

No one told a story quite like Tiger. Even if the tales had been embellished over the years, which they surely had been, they were still wonderful to hear and listen to because you knew the core of every story was true, and that was enough to leave you incredulous about what really went on inside NHL dressing rooms once upon a time.

I was looking forward to the game. I had been a little anxious before the game in Inuvik, but not this one. But I did feel like I was in the middle of a goal-scoring drought. If you counted the two games I had played with the Oldtimers the previous spring, this was my fourth game. I needed to score if for no other reason than to get the guys off my back.

"What do you say, guys?" Paul Reinhart asked the team. "If the rookie doesn't get a goal tonight, he's off the team."

"Absolutely," Gary Nylund chimed in. "We can't let him take up a roster spot if he's just going to float out there."

"Just stand by the net," Bob Rouse repeated. "I'll try and bank one in off you."

Johnny Bower appeared in the room to tell us the other team was on the ice for the warmups. The guys started putting on their helmets and grabbing their sticks and heading down the corridor to our bench, where we went out on the ice. Marcel Dionne was ahead of me, and as we headed out I was struck by the oddest feeling. I saw his namebar: Dionne. And his famous number, 16. And I couldn't believe that in half an hour I'd be in a game and this legend would again be my centre.

I laughed to myself. What would I tell my grandchildren one day? "Yep, Grandpa played with Marcel Dionne for a while. He wasn't a bad player at all. He set me up for more than a few." Well, I wouldn't be lying right up to the end. It was the "few" part that I was still working on. And since I wouldn't be in the lineup against Anchorage, this was my last chance on the northern swing of the Oldtimers tour. And I really wanted to get it here, with this group of guys, because we had become so close as a team in such a short period of time, and I knew that, despite their good-natured ribbing, they all desperately wanted me to score.

Of course, playing meant I had to be introduced again. And the guys all wondered what the announcer would say about me this time. "He works for a newspaper . . . and he's written stories . . . please welcome . . ." I had even suggested something funny to tour organizers like: "He once scored four goals for his atom house league team in Niagara Falls, Ontario, and now he's playing with the legends of hockey and writing a book about it. Please welcome . . ." But for some reason that didn't happen. So, as I waited for my name to be called, I could only cringe in anticipation.

"He's a sportswriter with the *Vancouver Sun* newspaper and he's writing a book . . ." And then the P.A. system started to crackle and you couldn't hear the rest of what the announcer was saying. Wouldn't that just be my luck? The one time it looked like they might get it right, and it cuts out just when my presence on this team would be explained so that I didn't look like some complete schmuck taking up a spot that could have gone to someone who played at least one game in the NHL. I was still some guy "writing a book," about what no one knew in Kenai knew. Oh well, maybe if I scored it would change all that.

Kenai had a couple of decent players, but not many. This game, despite a great effort by a rotation of goalies, would be over early. Dionne got us on the board early, and Wayne Babych got us a couple fairly quickly. Then Tiger followed behind him and the route was on. By the second period, the guys were trying to make the perfect play rather than run the score up to some ridiculous number.

While I had several assists after two periods of play, I was still without a goal. And now we were in the third period and guys were offering to give me extra shifts. Extra shifts were the last thing I needed, as I was staying out on the ice longer than I should have in an effort to get an extra chance, and as a result I was ending up at the bench violently grasping for breath. And it seemed that before I had a chance to catch it and allow my heart a chance to beat properly again, I was back out on the ice looking for that elusive goal.

There were three minutes left when Mark Lofthouse came to the bench on a change. I headed out with the play towards the enemy's end. I parked myself in the corner, near the faceoff circle, where I was fed the puck by one of our defencemen. I had no shot, so I spun around and started to head behind the other team's net. I don't know if the goalie thought I was going to shoot, or pass back to a teammate waiting in front of the net, but he stayed close to his post longer than I expected him to. So I continued behind the net with no one on me and suddenly found myself beside the other post with the puck on my stick. The goalie slid across but I managed to tuck the puck in just as he got there.

The puck crossed the line by two inches.

It wasn't the prettiest goal in the world. And because it wasn't immediately clear that the puck went in, my reaction and the ensuing celebration were delayed for a split second. But when it was obvious the puck had gone in and Ron Hoggarth went to fetch it for the faceoff at centre ice, my teammates began to surround me.

First Marcel Dionne, then Gary Nylund and Paul Reinhart. They were all putting me in headlocks and punching my arm. And when I looked up, I saw the rest of the team leap over the bench to congratulate me. It was a pretty amazing feeling, and I think the guys were genuinely happy for me. A part of me was happy for another reason—and this was really stupid—every time one of the Oldtimers scored a goal, he got to go the bench, grab a T-shirt autographed by the team, and then throw it into the stands. And no matter where we were, the crowd would go crazy trying to convince one of the guys to throw the shirt in their direction.

I wanted to throw one of those shirts into the crowd.

Now was my chance. I screamed around the bench and then looked up at the screaming masses. "What power," I mumbled to myself. Who would have thought a T-shirt could provoke such madness? I wanted this moment to last a lifetime, but they also had to get on with the game, so I found a particularly enthusiastic corner of the rink and fired the T-shirt over, producing a mad scramble on the other side. Then I skated to the bench with maybe the biggest smile I had ever worn. I had my goal. Life was good. And now I was officially one of the guys.

After the game was over, we gathered with the other team at centre ice for a photo. And this time I felt less like an imposter. I even imagined some player on the other team looking at the photo twenty years from now and pointing to me and saying, "Oh, did he score a beautiful goal on a wrap-around." Okay, maybe he wouldn't say that. But hopefully he wouldn't say: "I have no idea in hell who that is." Maybe he'd say, "I'm not sure who that is, but I think he played for the Sabres at one time." And who couldn't be happy with that?

In the dressing room after the game, the guys were happy for me. Tiger got everyone's attention.

"Guys, guys listen up," he said. "Tonight a very important milestone was reached by a teammate of ours. It may not have been a highlight-reel goal, but they all count. And so it is my great pleasure to present this puck to Gary Mason on the occasion of his first goal with the NHL Oldtimers."

He had the puck. I was so happy. I had asked Ron Hoggarth if I could have the puck near the end of the game. He had told me he'd thrown it into the crowd. Instead, he had it in his pocket, knowing that I'd want to hang on to it. Everyone crowded around me for a team picture with me and the puck. I put some tape on it that said: "First NHL Oldtimer goal. Kenai, Alaska. Nov. 11, 2001." I would have it mounted, I figured. Someone threw me a beer. "Here," my teammate said. "For once, you earned it."

I don't know if a beer ever tasted as sweet. I leaned back in my sweaty T-shirt with half my equipment still on and savoured every drop. I looked around, and all the guys were talking among themselves and beginning to untie skates and throw their gloves and elbow pads into their equipment bags. I wasn't in any such hurry. I could have sat there all night, I figured, had there been enough beer. But soon enough I was jolted back to reality.

"Our plane's leaving in forty-five minutes, so you'd better get your ass in gear," Jimmy Mann yelled over.

It was nice while it lasted. I frantically searched for the beginning of my sock tape so that I could start unravelling. I finally found it, and within minutes I was down to my shorts and heading for the shower. There was no hot water left by the time I got there, but it didn't matter.

"What are you smiling at?" Tiger said to me as I soaped up.

"Oh, nothing," I replied.

A few minutes later, I was throwing my clothes on and zipping up my hockey bag. Beside me my centreman was doing the same thing.

"You did good today," said Marcel Dionne, as I turned to grab my jacket.

"Thanks," I replied. "You did pretty good yourself."

Then we walked out of the room.

CHAPTER 7

SINGING CROCODILE ROCK

THE FLIGHT FROM KENAI to Anchorage took all
of twenty minutes. Still, it was just after ten o'clock
in the evening by the time we landed at our hotel,
the Millennium, which was quite grand and opulent when compared with most of the hotels we had stayed in during the trip.
The Millennium had leather chairs in the lobby, and oil paintings
hung on oak-panelled walls. It was the kind of place, in other
words, that the Oldtimers had been used to staying in during
their NHL days.

The high-end surroundings seemed to inspire the guys. While
most of us could have used a good night's sleep after the evening
at the Dog Sled, there was something faintly alluring about the
fact that we could sleep in the next day. This was the only time
on the trip that we had landed in a town the night before we were
to play there.

There was no way Tiger was heading anywhere. How he had
managed to even play in Kenai—and play so well—was a miracle

in itself. Marcel Dionne was heading to bed, as was Paul Rein-hart and anyone with the least amount of brains. That left myself, Russ Courtnall, Mark Lofthouse, Doug Bodger, Gary Nylund and Bob Rouse in the lobby trying to figure out where to go. The woman at the front desk suggested a bar called Koots, which wasn't that far away and had pretty good live music and cold beer.

Koots was four or five drinking establishments in one. Every time you turned a corner there was another room. We made our way to the back of the place, where a band called Ettinger was playing. Ettinger was one of those cover bands that could make a nice living in a place like Anchorage playing hits by Blink 182 and Offspring, Limp Bizkit and Linkin Park.

The lead singer had a toque pulled down over his long blond hair. He wore a nondescript T-shirt and camouflage fatigues. And he had a voice that could blow down a mountain. He was fabulous; he could sing anything. After a couple of beers, all us Old-timers began to get a second wind. Maybe it was the music that energized us and made us feel half our years. Whatever it was, we were glad to be here.

Before launching into another song, the band's lead singer, Peter Ettinger, introduced himself and the members of his group and said they all hailed from Vancouver, B.C. We all smiled broadly at one another. The fact that a Canadian was rockin' the joint seemed to make the night even better.

After the band finished its set and announced it was breaking for fifteen minutes, I wandered up to the stage to introduce myself to the lead singer. I thought he might be interested in knowing there was a group of compatriots in the audience who were thoroughly enjoying his music. I also figured that if he was any kind of hockey fan, he might get a kick out of the fact that Russ Courtnall and Doug Bodger were in the bar enjoying his music too.

As it turned out, Ettinger was a huge hockey fan and absolutely flipped when I informed him of who was in the bar.

"Could I meet them?" he asked.

"I think so," I replied.

I brought him over to where the guys were standing and introduced him to everyone. All of a sudden, this raging punker who was screaming obscenities into a microphone only minutes earlier was any seven-year-old kid from Canada meeting his first NHL hockey player.

"As soon as I finish tonight I'm phoning my dad," Ettinger told me. "He's not going to believe who I met. Russ Courtnall was my favourite player. I loved him. And Bob Rouse, God, I watched him win a Stanley Cup two years ago. This is unbelievable. This is the highlight of my life."

The singer told us about the incredible gig his band had landed in Anchorage. They played at Koots twenty-six weeks of the year and made off like bandits. All in U.S. dollars. It allowed him and his band members to enjoy a very comfortable middle-class existence back in Vancouver, one of the most expensive cities in North America. Equally amazing was the fact that this guy was in his early forties. First, he didn't look it. Second, he could jump around a stage with the energy of someone half his age.

Ettinger returned to the stage to play another set, while Russ Courtnall plotted.

"We should get him in the game tomorrow," Courtnall said to the guys. "It would absolutely be the thrill of his life."

"He can use my stuff," I blurted out. "He would just need skates."

"What would Tiger say?" said Gary Nylund.

"Tiger will be fine with it," said Courtnall. "But we'll run it by him."

During the set, Ettinger invited Doug Bodger up on stage to sing. He and Ettinger talked for a minute about what song Bodger might do, and they decided on "Crocodile Rock" by Elton John. And ten seconds later Bodge was off, tapping his toe on the floor, slapping his leg with his free hand, remembering when rock was young and he and Susie had so much fun.

The guys were in stitches in the back of the room. We couldn't believe where Bodger found the nerve to perform in public the way he did, but he clearly loved it. He was a natural ham who had a voice to back up his ambitions—although, compared with the lithe Ettinger and most rock singers, Bodger was an unusual sight. He was built like a middle linebacker and had thighs the size of thirty-pound turkeys. His hands were so big that it looked like he was holding a TV remote, not a microphone. But he loved it, belting out lyric after lyric while people crowded the dance floor in front of him. This was better than karaoke could ever be.

Bodger wrapped up his number with enthusiastic cheering from the mostly twenty-something crowd, who were completely unaware that a former NHL hockey player was on the stage, although they might have been puzzled by his hefty physique. Bodger got a pat on the back from Ettinger and then made it to the back, where the boys had a round waiting for him. He was so pumped that he ordered his own round of shooters for the guys. Suddenly the scene at the Dog Sled Saloon the night before was a distant memory.

After Ettinger finished his second set, he came back to talk to the guys. He arrived to discover that Courtnall had a proposition: "How would you like to play with us tomorrow night?"

"You're joking, right?" replied Ettinger.

"No, we're serious," Courtnall continued. "You can use Gary's equipment. You said you had skates, so all you need to do is bring those. We have lots of sticks. That's it. You're all set."

"Oh, my God," Ettinger smiled. "I can't believe you're serious. That would be the biggest honour, the biggest thrill of my entire life. I can't believe you're serious."

"We're serious. So you're in?"

"I'm in if you want me."

This time it was Ettinger's turn to buy the round, which he did, to the lingering doubt of some of us who were now beginning to lose that second wind we had found earlier. It was now 2:30 A.M., and the guys were all in favour of hitting the hay. We finished up our drinks and gave Ettinger a number to call to get details on where we were playing and when he should be there.

"I can't thank you enough," he said as we left.

The next morning was clear and bright, unlike the dispositions of those of us who had stayed out too late the night before. I wandered down to the restaurant around noon to see if there were any stragglers from breakfast still about. Tiger and his wife, Brenda, were there, and a few others, but none of the gang who were at Koots not that many hours earlier.

Sitting down with Tiger was perfect. He did all the talking. I was always surprised when I talked to Tiger, mostly by all the information he had stored in that odd-shaped head of his. If you didn't know he was a famous hockey player, he could be any farmer from the prairies with his tattered trucker's cap and deep-rooted crow's feet. Tiger looked like he'd lived life hard and, I suppose, he had. For most of his fourteen seasons in the NHL he traded punches with the toughest players in the game, racking up more penalty minutes—3,966—than anyone who has ever played in the NHL.

He'd taken sticks to the face, throat, gut and back of the legs and dished out just as many. He played each game like it was his last. But while he looked and sounded like a character in the satirical hockey movie, *Slap Shot*, Williams's goofball, knuckle-dragging persona was in many ways an act, I was discovering. There was a lot more to the Weyburn, Saskatchewan, brawler than anyone knew.

After we finished lunch that day, Brenda decided to go for a walk and enjoy a resplendent Anchorage afternoon. Tiger and I hung out at the table, accepting coffee refill after coffee refill, talking about his days as a kid growing up on the prairies, then sharing a dressing room with Darryl Sittler and Lanny McDonald and finally, sadly, having to call it quits. Williams seldom showed a tender or vulnerable side, but when he talked about what hockey meant to him and how difficult it was to have to say goodbye to it, the timbre of his voice changed and his sentences became shorter. After all these years it still hurt.

"Those early years in Toronto, Brenda and I didn't have much money," Williams said, laughing at the thought. "I was one of the few guys who had eighty per cent of his salary diverted into deferred annuities so I would be guaranteed money when I retired. Most of the guys when they first broke into the league just went out and blew the money because it was the first time they had cash like that.

"I remember guys were buying full-length mink coats and new cars and fancy homes, not me. Because I had so much of my salary put away, Brenda and I lived on a real tight budget, and I mean real tight. We lived in this tiny little house, just tiny, and I bought a '64 Oldsmobile with seventy thousand miles on it. Get this. It was so ugly the Leafs didn't want me parking it in the players lot, so I had to park it with the employees. But our budget was so tight that by the end of August we literally had no money left. We were just waiting for the start of the season so we could get our cheques coming in again."

Their frugality would pay off. Today, Williams doesn't worry about money, as his NHL pension and the money he put away early in his career provides him with a comfortable lifestyle, which includes a beautiful home in West Vancouver and a lodge-style villa in the ski resort of Whistler. He also earns tens of thousands of dollars playing hockey in exhibition tours like the one we were on, plus others, as well as earning a substantial income from his oil and gas exploration company. Not bad for someone who used to get five cents for every gopher and five dollars for every magpie he shot growing up as a kid in Weyburn.

It's no surprise that Williams was as tough as he was when you heard him talk about growing up, particularly about being coached by his dad, Taffy. Taffy Williams was a no-nonsense farmer who raised his six boys in his image. Although he had never worn a pair of skates in his life, he still coached the boys' hockey teams, yelling instructions from the bench. And if you ever wondered where Tiger inherited his competitive fire and his cutthroat, win-at-all-cost approach to hockey, you didn't need to look any further than Taffy.

"My dad was a mean son of a bitch," Williams said, not cracking a smile. "During games he would intimidate the players on the other team. Some guy would skate by our bench and he'd yell out: 'Better keep your head up, 16, because your time is coming.' And that was the signal for someone sitting on our bench to take care of Number 16 the next time he was on the ice."

Often that person was Tiger himself.

As you listened to Williams talk about some of his father's motivational techniques, you could only laugh. Someone trying the same stunts today might be thrown in jail or lynched in the town square by an angry mob of hockey moms. For instance, when Tiger was thirteen, his peewee team was quite a success. And with each win, the coach's expectations grew.

"If we lost, Dad would be so mad he'd lose it," Williams said. "He wouldn't turn the heat on in the bus on the way home from wherever we were coming from. And this is in the dead of winter, and it's twenty below outside. Or the other trick he'd like to pull was to stop the bus about a mile outside of town and let us walk the rest of the way. The parents would go nuts, eh, but if they complained Dad would just say, 'If you don't like it then take your son off the team, we don't want him.'"

Taffy Williams could be ingenious too.

Tiger remembered one time when that same team of thirteen-year-olds was playing in the western final on an outdoor rink.

It was a particularly harsh prairie afternoon, and the wind blew the wind chill factor to nearly thirty below. It was weather barely fit for polar bears, let alone young kids, but the game went on. Knowing the conditions could be a factor in the outcome, Taffy Williams decided to borrow extra goalie gear for the game. Ten sets to be exact. No one could quite figure out what he had in mind until just before the game when he outlined his strategy.

"My dad figured that if we left one goalie out there for the whole time he'd be frozen after five minutes and wouldn't be able to move," Williams said that afternoon. "So, he thought he'd give everyone a chance to go in, and by rotating kids through the position our goalie would always be relatively warm and fresh."

The strategy worked to perfection.

Still, Williams's best stories were from his days in the NHL, where he was a main attraction in every building he entered. As someone who usually forgot a person's name five seconds after being introduced, I had nothing but respect for Williams's amazing powers of recall. He could remember the circumstances that preceded a fight he got into in the twenty-third game of his fifth season in the league. And, of course, he told his stories with such flare and enthusiasm that it was hard not to be amazed. He had packed so much into his forty-eight years on earth that it was hard not to applaud his zest for life.

All you had to do, it seemed, was mention a player's name and Williams had a story, or twenty, involving the player. And so it was when his friend Curt Fraser's name came up while we were talking. Fraser was one of Williams's teammates in Vancouver, and I remembered reading at the time that Tiger was extremely upset the day his buddy was traded by the Canucks to the Chicago Blackhawks.

"Oh, Christ, I was pissed," said Williams, sounding like he was still mad. "We were on the road, and I remember I didn't take the team bus to the rink. I was so mad at what they'd done. I remember Roger Neilson, who was our coach then, asking me if I'd take the new kid we were getting in the trade, Tony Tanti, under my arm and help him because he was young and was going to need a veteran to show him the ropes.

"Well, Tanti wore 22 in junior and that's where he was coming from, so when he arrived all his sticks had 22 on the top of them. Well, I saw that and decided to have some fun with it. I had Ronnie Delorme call all the guys together for a team meeting. So he gets everybody in the room and then I come in carrying all these sticks and threw them on the floor, just scaring the shit out of everybody.

"Okay, who had my number put on their sticks? Which one of you is going to have the guts to fess up? And then I went around the room: 'Was it you, Gradin?' Was it you, so and so. Of course, everyone denies it was them or that the sticks were theirs. So I finish by vowing to find the guy, and when I did he was going to be dead."

Twenty minutes later, according to Williams, Tanti was found cutting off the tops of his hockey sticks.

Of the four NHL teams that he would play for, Williams admitted that the biggest piece of his heart was owned by the Leafs. Hockey in Hogtown was just so much bigger than it was anywhere else. But his days as a Canuck, in those ugly orange, black and yellow O Henry uniforms, were pretty special too, he admitted. The predicaments he often found himself in with his teammates from those days were something that would bond them for life.

Like the night the Canucks were visiting Hartford to play the since-relocated Whalers, and the team went out to a local bar called The Russian Lady after the game. As Williams recalled, some of the guys on the team were throwing ice around the joint when someone got hit who didn't like it, and the next thing you knew a brawl erupted. Police arrived and arrested three members of the team. Tiger, who'd had a few along with his teammates, decided to head down to the police station, hoping a little fast-talking might set his buddies free.

"So, I show up at the station and I guess they thought I was getting too mouthy, which I probably was, so a few cops take me downstairs, handcuff me to the bars of one of the jails and then proceed to beat the living shit out of me," Williams remembered. "It was bad. They beat me up pretty good. It was right out of a movie, with each guy taking a turn at giving it to me."

Eventually, they let Williams go and he staggered back to the Canucks' hotel, where he immediately set about trying to raise enough bail money to get the three Canucks free. It was three o'clock in the morning when Williams started knocking on people's doors, ordering them to fish as much money out of their wallets as they could. Most co-operated, but a few were reluctant to part with their hard-earned dollars.

"I remember Thomas Gradin wasn't going to give me any money," Williams laughs. "He was a tight bastard. I grabbed him by the collar and said, 'Listen, you little son of a bitch. You'd better give me every red cent you have or I'm going to plow you, understand?' He went off and got some money, but boy was I pissed at him."

Williams, I figured, could have spent all afternoon and night telling stories. He could have done so for forty days and forty nights straight, and still he wouldn't have exhausted his supply of tales from his NHL days. There probably wouldn't be another player like him, you couldn't help but think when you listened to him or saw him carrying on with his teammates or some unsuspecting member of the public. Williams certainly had his detractors. A long list of former opponents would readily say he was one of the dirtiest players in the league. But an equally long list of teammates would tell you that he'd do anything for you and that if you had to go into battle, you wanted Williams on your side rather than against you.

Although he wasn't in the Hockey Hall of Fame, Williams was the star of this show. Every time he scored a goal and rode his stick down the ice like he used to with the Leafs and the Canucks, fans ate it up. Every time the public entered the dressing room for autographs and pictures, Williams's stall was always the busiest.

"Tiger," said one man. "I always loved the way you played the game. You weren't the best, but you gave it your best every time you were out there. And I just wanted to say thanks."

Williams seemed surprised by the high praise, even a little embarrassed. And for the first time on the trip he was almost at a loss for words.

"Thanks," was all he could muster.

THE GAME AGAINST the Anchorage Aces was about an hour away. The Oldtimers' special guest, Peter Ettinger, had arrived, clearly excited and almost in a state of shock as he looked around to see himself sharing a dressing room with Richard Brodeur and Marcel Dionne. He would look at me and smile, shake his head and continue putting on the equipment I had loaned him.

With about twenty minutes to go before the Oldtimers were scheduled to go on the ice for the pre-game warmup, a few of the guys decided to have some fun with the new recruit.

"I hope this game doesn't become a bloodbath like the last time we played them," Jimmy Mann announced to the room. "What was there? Ten fights the last time we played them. The crowd loved it, but they've brought in some real bad guys this time around I heard, so they might do anything."

Suddenly, the ever-present smile on Peter Ettinger's face disappeared. He was all ears.

Tiger came in from another room, where some of the players were dressing. "Jimmy," he said to Mann. "Do my hands for me."

Mann grabbed some white hockey tape from his bag and started wrapping it around Williams's right fist, the way a fighter gets his hands done before a bout.

"Remember, he sucker-punched you last time, Tiger," Mann said. "You've got to get that prick back. Don't hold back."

"Oh, I'll get him," Williams replied. "But I'm worried that the same thing is going to happen as last time. Remember?"

"You mean the bench-clearing brawl?"

"Yep, I bet that's what will happen tonight."

As Williams and Mann performed their routine to perfection, a certain singer who couldn't sleep the night before, who was so excited about his chance to play with his boyhood heroes, sat in stony silence. All the joy that he entered the room with seemed to have been sucked from his body. Where once he envisioned jubilantly raising his arms after scoring a goal, now he imagined being somebody's punching bag.

The worst part was that the boys knew they had the poor rookie right where they wanted him.

"Are the cops in the building?" asked Bob Rouse. "Can someone go check? This could get real ugly, and I just want to make sure we get out of here alive."

Ron Hoggarth, the referee, had been made aware of what was going on in the room. And it was just too good a party to pass up.

"Okay, guys," Hoggarth said, entering the dressing room without the smile normally pasted on his face. "I understand that Moran kid is dressed for the other team. This is the kid who was suspended from the West Coast league, suspended from the AHL, suspended from the East Coast league. He's basically a headhunter. Do we play with him in the lineup or not?"

"We damn well play," Mann immediately chimed in.

"Oh, yeah," said Rouse. "We play and that asshole is dead."

Then he looked at Ettinger.

"I don't think it's a good idea to wear a visor," he said, inspecting the helmet of mine that Ettinger was intending to use. "You can if you want, but if you get punched in the head and that glass shatters, it could really mess up your face. And there's a good chance you're going to have to fight tonight, so I'd take it off if I were you. Does anyone have a screwdriver?"

As Ettinger looked helplessly on, Rouse began disassembling the visor on Ettinger's helmet. Now I started to feel sorry for the guy. The hour before the game should have been a time he enjoyed, not a time he felt like puking. But as the guys' little prank went on, that's exactly what Peter Ettinger looked like he would soon do—all over the dressing room floor. But if you thought the Oldtimers would eventually take pity on the poor guy and relent, let him in on their gag, you could forget it. These were athletes who were taught that when you had someone down, you stepped on him even harder to make sure he didn't get up. And that included poor schmucks getting taken in by a sophomoric prank.

Gary Nylund came into the room and asked if anyone had any Vaseline he could put on his face, like boxers did before fights. They did this to make their faces harder to split open. Someone threw a tube to Nylund, who started putting the cream on his face before passing it around to the others.

The closer it got to the pre-game warmup, the more worked up the guys got.

"Come on, let's kill those bastards!" yelled Rouse. "Let's pound the living shit out of them."

"Don't take any crap, guys," Mann followed. "Let's stick up for one another out there, even if it means squaring off with that psycho."

"You ready?" Rouse said, looking over at Ettinger.

"Yeah," Ettinger said softly. "I think so."

"Look," Rouse continued. "If you get into trouble and some-one starts pounding on you, just cover your head and hit the ice until one of us gets there to help you out. But you know, if you can give the guy a couple of shots before you go down, that would be great too."

"And another thing," Mann instructed Ettinger before heading out of the ice. "If any of them gives you a dirty look during the warm-up, you just look right back at them and say, 'What're you looking at, asshole?' Okay? Make sure they know you're not afraid of anything and that you're ready to go if they are."

The Oldtimers headed out on the ice with one scared rock singer in their midst. Jimmy Mann had gone out ahead of time and spoken with the biggest guy on the Anchorage team and filled him in on what the Oldtimers were doing to their new recruit. Mann encouraged the guy to "have words" with Ettinger before the game if their paths crossed near the red line. And sure enough they did, as the two teams skated around, taking shots on their goalies. The player Mann had teed up for the encounter gave Ettinger the shoulder, shouting: "You been talking shit about me?" Well, you should have seen the look on Peter Ettinger's face. "No," he told the player. "I haven't said anything about you." "We'll see, bigmouth," said the Anchorage goon, just before Mann arrived on the scene to push the player away. "We'll take care of this during the game," Mann barked.

Ettinger tried to concentrate the best he could for the remainder of the warm-up, but he didn't look like he was really into it. His shots were half-hearted, and he seemed to spend most of the time sizing up the opposition. The gag, however, was about to reach its climax.

Rouse had asked me to get a towel and as many packets of ketchup as I could find in the arena. He was going to wait for the Oldtimers to return to the dressing room following the warmup, and then I would meet him when he got off the ice and help him with the old ketchup-as-blood routine. I caught Ettinger as he was coming off the ice and quickly asked him about the altercation at centre ice.

"What was that all about?" I asked.

"He apparently thought I'd said something about him," Ettinger said, with not even a hint of a smile.

"Do you want to go through with this?" I asked.

Ettinger paused.

"I think so."

He continued into the dressing room, and I waited for Rouse.

"Get the ketchup?"

"Yep."

"Okay," said Rouse. "Smear some on my face and put a bunch in the towel, and then I'll go into the dressing room with the towel up to my face."

So there I was, laughing hysterically, as I put ketchup all over Bob Rouse's face, trying to pull off one of the oldest tricks in the books.

"How's it look?" Rouse asked.

"Great," I said. "Now, let me get to the room first. I wouldn't miss this for the world."

By the time I got to the dressing room, things were quiet. Most of the guys were evaluating the tape on their hands and punching their fists into the palms of their hand. I took a seat across from the target of this elaborate charade to catch his reaction when Rouse entered the room—which he did, seconds later.

"The asshole sucker-punched me!" Rouse screamed, as the door to the dressing room was flung open and a hockey stick crashed against a bank of sticks against the wall.

Rouse was holding the towel to his face, under his right eye, but there was enough red on the towel that you immediately thought blood had been spilled.

"Which guy?" Jimmy Mann asked.

"The big guy, Number 10," Rouse said. "Then he took right off. I'm going to kill him when I get out there."

"What happened?" Tiger said, rushing into the room.

"Number 10 suckered Bobby."

"Okay, boys," Williams shouted out. "They want a war, they're going to get a war. Sharpen your sticks fellas, because there's going to be a whole lot of carving going on out there."

I thought Peter Ettinger was going to faint. What the hell had he got himself into, he must have thought. How had such a wonderful dream turned into such a god-awful nightmare? His head was mostly hung down now. He didn't even want to look up. Any time he did lift his head, it was to take deep breaths. What he wouldn't give, I imagined him thinking, to be back on the stage singing something by Creed or Lifehouse right now.

Rouse took his seat in the room right beside Ettinger. Little did Rouse know it was a move that would ultimately expose the group's madcap caper.

"After a while," Ettinger would reveal later, "I got a whiff of this smell. And it was one that smelled distinctly like ketchup. I've had enough fries in my life to know what ketchup smells like, and I put two and two together and realized they had been stringing me along. And you have no idea how happy and relieved I was to find out that it was just ketchup."

And that was how Peter Ettinger came to discover that his life hadn't really been in danger after all. He had simply been had, for close to an hour, by a savvy group of former NHL stars who never passed up an opportunity to exploit some poor unsuspecting soul in order to generate a few laughs.

When it was time for the pre-game introductions, Peter Ettinger, singer, strode out on the ice with a whole new sense of purpose. He could smile again and enjoy what he would later describe as the greatest thrill of his life. He wouldn't score a goal, but it didn't matter. He was playing alongside Marcel Dionne and Russ Courtnall, and he would have pictures to prove it.

The Oldtimers would roll over the Anchorage Aces, the team's toughest opponent, and when it was over everyone assembled at centre ice for a picture. In the front, wearing the biggest smile, was this mop of blond hair.

"I can't thank you enough," Peter Ettinger said to me after getting dressed. "If you hadn't loaned me the equipment, I couldn't have played."

"No problem," I said. "Was it everything you thought it would be?"

Ettinger beamed. "I'll never forget this night for the rest of my life."

CHAPTER 8

MARVELLOUS MARCEL

IT'S STRANGE WHEN a team breaks up. Even one
that's been together for only a week.

But that's what happens on the Oldtimers tour.
No one does it forever, because of jobs and other commitments.
So, as the tour headed south, dipping into the Lower Mainland
of British Columbia and then into the Interior and parts of the
north, some guys on the team were leaving and new guys were
coming aboard.

In seven wonderful days our Oldtimers team had become remarkably close, which is what can happen when you get a group
of people together for a common cause—and you have plenty of
beer to fortify your spirits along the way. But I sensed genuine
regret among the guys that this portion of the tour was coming to
an end and that six of the guys, plus Johnny Bower, would be
returning to their homes and other lives, to be replaced by a new
group of players and by Bobby Hull, who would take Johnny's
place as honorary coach and chief autograph signer.

Russ Courtnall was returning to Los Angeles, where he and his wife, Paris Vaughan, daughter of the late jazz singer Sarah Vaughan, lived with their two children and where he often passed his days on golf courses with his buddy, Wayne Gretzky. Bob Rouse was returning to Langley, B.C., where he and his family owned a sprawling farm. Rouse was still adjusting to life after hockey, had loads of money and was seemingly in no hurry to race into another career. Doug Bodger was living on Vancouver Island, where he ran a sports store near Duncan. The store, he said, was more for something to do than anything else, but his real joy was helping to coach a junior hockey team with former NHL player Greg Adams.

Mark Lofthouse also lived in Langley, where he had become a successful real estate agent. Paul Reinhart, meantime, was returning to West Vancouver to look after a professional lacrosse team, the Vancouver Ravens, that he had become part-owner of, as well as keeping his eye out for other potential investment opportunities. Richard Brodeur was returning to Vancouver, where he was the general manager of a couple of high-end hotels. And Johnny Bower was returning to Toronto, where he would be spotted in the crowd during nationally televised home games of the Leafs. He would split his time between his home there and a place he had down in Florida.

As we waited for our plane in the Whitehorse airport, the guys reminisced about the past week. About sending kids for buckets of steam and scaring the daylights out of rock singers. Maybe this wasn't the NHL, but in some ways it was no different from the hundreds of road trips these players had taken in their lives. At the end of it they had the same thing they would have at the end of any road trip during their playing days—stories. And laughs that they would share with one another when their paths crossed again, someday down the road.

"That was such a blast," said Russ Courtnall, who many were so surprised to see on an Oldtimers tour.

When we landed in Vancouver, all of us exchanged numbers. Mark Lofthouse, who had taken the most pictures on the far north swing, promised to send guys prints of the best shots he had. Everyone vowed to do it again next year. And then people started to head off in different directions, resuming their lives.

The Oldtimers tour, meantime, had to roll on. Replacements rolled in for the remaining stops on this tour of the far north and western Canada. And although many of the players had distinctly western roots, they were players who had played everywhere.

The new team really became a team when the tour stopped in the beautiful B.C. Interior city of Kelowna, where the new recruits were joined by the team's new coach, Bobby Hull. The players included Garth Butcher, a rugged defenceman who had played his junior hockey in Regina and fourteen seasons and a notable 897 games in the NHL. He had worn the uniforms of the Vancouver Canucks, St. Louis Blues, Quebec Nordiques and Toronto Maple Leafs.

Also joining the blueline corps was Jiri Bubla. The Czech-born defenceman had played only five years in the NHL but many more years professionally in Europe. All of his NHL time was spent with the Vancouver Canucks. After hockey, Bubla ran into trouble with the law, spending time in jail for drug trafficking. Since getting out of jail, he had worked hard to turn his life around, starting a janitorial company. In fact, he got a contract to clean the very NHL arena he had once played in—Pacific Coliseum. Bubla's selection to the team was a case of Tiger doing something nice for a former teammate who had worked hard to make things right again.

Also at the back end was Doug Lidster. Lidster had spent sixteen years in the NHL, long enough to win two Stanley Cups along the way. Those Cup wins came during his time with the Rangers and a brief stop at the tail end of his career with the Dallas Stars. But Lidster had also spent time in Vancouver and St. Louis, where he established a reputation as a smooth skater who was steady and dependable.

Up front, the new recruits included some old faces. At sixty-six years of age, Orland Kurtenbach was the senior citizen of the tour and someone who genuinely fit the description of an Old-timer. The first-ever captain of the Canucks, Kurtenbach had a successful thirteen-year career in the NHL that also saw him spend time in New York (with the Rangers), Boston and Toronto. He may have had a full head of grey hair, but he still knew his way around an ice rink.

Also playing forward was Tony Tanti. An eleven-year NHL veteran with Chicago, Pittsburgh, Buffalo and Vancouver, and three times a forty-goal-or-more goal scorer, Tanti finished his professional hockey playing days in Europe. He spent six seasons playing in Germany before returning to Canada, where he, like many of his former Canucks teammates, had settled in Vancouver.

In goal, meantime, was Bill Ranford. The two-time Stanley Cup winner who was named winner of the Conn Smythe in the 1989–90 playoffs, Ranford had made quite a name for himself in his fifteen NHL seasons. Ranford started out playing goal in Boston but had his best years in an Edmonton Oilers uniform, where he won both of his Cups. Along the way he also played in Washington, Tampa and Detroit, before wrapping up his career back in Edmonton.

And then there was Bobby Hull, who had become a mainstay on the Oldtimers tour. He no longer laced up his skates and played, but he didn't need to in order to attract crowds. Most nights, all he had to do was set up shop in the concourse of whichever arena we happened to be in, and parents and kids would flock to him to get him to sign some old picture of Hull they'd had for years or, when desperate, any old scrap of paper they happened to have with them.

In person, Hull was much shorter than I remembered him being when he played in the NHL and later in the World Hockey Association. But then, when you're a kid, every NHL hockey player seems larger than life. And in his playing days Hull was as big as they came. Since retiring in 1980, he had spent most of his time in the Chicago area, where he still owned a home. He dabbled in a few businesses and investment opportunities and still did the odd commercial, but none of it had made Hull a rich man. So he was always anxious to get on the Oldtimers tour, where he could make a few bucks selling autographed photos of himself, as well as other personalized memorabilia, at the postgame receptions.

Although most of the players on our newly configured team knew each other from their time in the NHL, it would take some time to feel completely comfortable as a team. Many of the new guys were anxious to know how the earlier games had gone, what places like Inuvik and Kenai were like. And, naturally, there was some catching up to do—the players asked about the well-being and whereabouts of old teammates or acquaintances they had in common. What was clear, however, was that all of the guys at one time belonged to the same exclusive club—the NHL—and in that they had a bond that tied them together and made any awkward first moments disappear in a hurry.

In Kelowna, the Oldtimers were playing at Skyreach Place, a modern junior hockey arena that sat about 6,500 but had the look and feel of an NHL rink, only smaller. It had corporate boxes and cushioned seats. Tickets for a Rod Stewart concert in the building had sold out in an hour at prices ranging from $84 to $140. After entertaining crowds at the Midnight Sun recreation arena in Inuvik and the Big Dipper Arena in Fairbanks, playing at Skyreach Place was a bit of a treat.

We were staying at The Coast, one of Kelowna's more established and better-known hotels. Marcel Dionne and I had been meaning to get together to chat, and the three hours we had to kill before game time seemed like the perfect opportunity.

I had observed a lot of Dionne in dressing rooms and on

planes and buses, but I still didn't feel I knew him very well. He had kept to himself somewhat during the northern swing. He'd had his fill, he would say, of bars and late nights, and at fifty years of age what he needed most was sleep. Which was fair enough. Still, I couldn't help feeling there was something else going on.

You sometimes got the feeling that Dionne thought he was just a little bit better than the rest of the guys in the group. That his Hockey Hall of Fame credentials put him a notch above Wayne Babych and Doug Bodger and even guys who had won Stanley Cups, like Bob Rouse. During his days in the NHL, Dionne made no secret of the fact that he felt he didn't get nearly the respect and attention that his achievements warranted. Consequently, he played the game with a bit of a chip on his shoulder. Sometimes, it seemed like that chip was still there.

When I had played with the Oldtimers earlier, Dionne was one of the first players I met. He wasn't particularly friendly, and when a spot was open beside him in the dressing room I hesitated to plunk myself down. He seemed ornery, and maybe his hawk-like features, a small face dominated by a nose that went out and then took a sharp curve down, made him seem more unfriendly. However, this time around he didn't seem nearly as intimidating as he did on the earlier trip. He was smiling a lot more, chatting with the guys more than I remembered from the previous time, and yet below the surface I sensed something was still simmering. I wanted to find out what it was.

When you look at the list of Dionne's accomplishments, they are truly amazing. He was Detroit's first draft choice, second overall, in 1971. In eighteen seasons, mostly spent with the often-mediocre Los Angeles Kings, Dionne scored 731 goals and recorded 1,771 points, third highest in NHL history. Along the way he won two Lady Byng trophies as the league's most gentlemanly player and a Pearson award as the league's best player, as voted by the players themselves. In 1980, he won the Art Ross

Trophy as the league's leading scorer. He played in eight All-Star games, and six times he scored 50 goals or more, four times 40 or more and fourteen times 30 or more.

But he never won a Stanley Cup.

And that fact, many believe, hurt Dionne more than any other when it came to acknowledging his greatness and his ultimate place in the pantheon of the NHL's biggest stars. The truly great players led their team to the Stanley Cup, it was said. Dionne didn't. Not that he didn't try—in some cases too hard, some hockey experts argued. One of the biggest knocks against Dionne was that he tried to do too much himself and consequently hurt the Kings more often than helped them. Others looked at it differently, accusing Dionne of being a selfish player who cared more about himself and his personal statistics than about team success. Dionne had heard the same charges during his career and always bristled when he did. "That's a bunch of crap," he would say. And would add: "I'm the third-highest scorer in the NHL, and they can't take that away from me."

Hockey was a business, nothing more. That's what Dionne learned early in his career.

"When I was in Detroit," Dionne said, shortly after we sat down for coffee, "I saw what they did to Gordie Howe. I saw how they shuffled him aside like he was nothing. Well, I'll tell you, I was only twenty at the time and that changed me for good. I realized you had to look out for yourself. Nobody can predict how long you are going to play. One bad injury and it's all over.

"I learned early that money was very, very important. I was not going to sit back and just go along with things. That's why I left Detroit. There were different reasons, but the people who couldn't accept my leaving the most were the players. The guys were pissed at me, and yet when I went to L.A. all of a sudden the rest of the guys started to make more money."

Dionne was right. The Red Wing players were angry at him

for leaving an organization that had wanted to make him its cornerstone. Was there no loyalty anymore? Dionne was one of the first players to use new flexibility in the players' collective agreement with the owners to cash in on a lucrative offer from another team. But because this was so rare in the 1970s, many players resented Dionne for seemingly selling out to the highest bidder. But Dionne had no time for those who wanted to carp behind his back. All the finger-pointing in Dionne's direction only made him stronger.

"Look," he said, setting down his coffee. "This is a business. People say it's all about the love of the game. Well, that's over-rated, and frankly it's bullshit. It's a question of making a living, realizing it's a business and, once you're finished, deciding what you're going to do for yourself."

What do you make of a statement like that? It sounds so crass, so me-first, which was the attitude hockey players deplored most in those who played the game. And when I later thought about it, I couldn't help thinking this was exactly the kind of re-mark that helped establish Dionne's reputation among many players as a mercenary, someone who was out for himself first and his team second. But was that fair? Was what he was saying all that far off the mark?

It might have been thirty or forty years ago when there wasn't that much money in the game. But certainly in the last ten or twenty years, money was a motivating force for a whole new gen-eration of players. This notion of men playing in the NHL for the "love of the game" was pretty antiquated nowadays. Hockey, thanks to players, their union, the owners, marketing people, the Internet age—a whole host of factors—had made the game a business first and a sport second. And while it might not have sounded good when blurted out loud, what Dionne was telling me was the absolute truth.

He began to talk about his time in a Los Angeles Kings uniform. The Kings, of course, would be the team on which Dionne would be united with Dave Taylor and Charlie Simmer to form the Triple Crown line. Throughout the 1980s, this line would be one of the most prolific in the NHL. And yet, for all its success and for all of Dionne's personal glory, L.A. never won a Stanley Cup while he was there, and the fact that the City of Angels was pretty much an NHL backwater whose games ended when most of the East was fast asleep made it easy to overlook the efforts of some of the team's players. Which was another way of saying that Dionne never got the respect his numbers merited. But according to Dionne, the Kings didn't do much to help their cause either.

"The managers and owners in L.A. were idiots," Dionne said, as the waitress came to offer us a refill. "They never focussed on how to promote the game at all. As for me, I probably would have been a better second-line centre than first-line because of my size, and nobody understood that. I was only five-foot-seven, and I had to always go up against the other team's top line.

"Now it made me stronger. You learned to survive. But we had bad management—horrible management—and as a result our franchise never had a chance to be successful."

One of the owners during the period, Jack Kent Cooke, would often overrule the team's GM, Bob Pulford, on trades. Every season was like a revolving door. It wasn't unusual, said Dionne, for thirty players to suit up for the Kings over the course of a season. The one piece that was always missing, according to Dionne, was a puck-moving defenceman. It was one luxury Dionne never had, and there is nothing that can help an offence more than someone who can lug the puck out of his end and head-man the puck to a centreman breaking up through the middle. Dionne could only shake his head at the thought of how many more goals he might have scored, how many more wins the Kings might have racked up, if they'd had a Larry Robinson, or a Denis Potvin or a Paul Coffey, on their blueline during the prime of the Triple Crown line.

"I probably would have scored nine hundred goals," Dionne said, without a hint of humour. "I played with those guys (Robinson, Potvin) at the World Championships and at Canada Cups and All-Star games. It's a joke what a difference it makes. How easy it was. I didn't play with guys who could make the first pass. When I got it, the puck was always in the back of my skates. We spent a lot of time trying to reorganize our attacks because the passes were never there."

As Dionne talked, I could only imagine the reaction of some of his teammates, specifically some of the defencemen he played with, when they read it. It sure wouldn't do anything to endear him to his former teammates. But that was Marcel. I'd never met anyone, aside perhaps from Tiger, who didn't care what others thought of him. The fact that some of his old playing partners might be offended by his description of their abilities didn't even faze Dionne.

In our conversation, I began to notice how often Dionne used the word respect. And more often than not it would be preceded with the words, lack of. This was a recurring theme, and it was easy to detect a vein of bitterness running through him. When you looked at his résumé, you could certainly see moments where Dionne probably shook his head in disgust. Like his very first year in the NHL, 1971–72.

Dionne set a rookie scoring record with 77 points, yet he ended up trailing both Montreal goaltender Ken Dryden and Buffalo winger Rick Martin in voting for the Calder Trophy as the league's top rookie.

In 1979–80, Dionne had 137 points to tie rookie Wayne Gretzky for the league lead. However, Dionne was awarded the Art Ross Trophy for most points because he had more goals than Gretzky—53 to 51. But despite edging out Gretzky for the selection as centre on the first All-Star team, it was clear that the lithe centre from the Edmonton Oilers had captured the imagination of hockey fans everywhere and in the process had overshadowed Dionne's accomplishments. Maybe that was more a case of poor timing than anything else. Yet, Dionne couldn't help but wonder why he had to share his moment in the sun with a long-haired, bony-kneed teenager from Brampton who was just starting his NHL journey while Dionne was ending his.

On March 10, 1987, Dionne was traded by the Kings to the New York Rangers. The Kings decided to trade their best player while they could still get something for him. Dionne had scored 126 points two seasons earlier, and 94 points the year before, and he had compiled 74 points on 24 goals and 50 assists at the time of the trade. So it was not like he was an old man who had completely lost his touch. But if Dionne thought things were bad in Los Angeles in terms of management, he hadn't seen anything yet.

"I only played, I think, fourteen games that first season in New York," Dionne said, as he began to recount the final chapter of his illustrious career. "Well, when I got there, things were totally out of control. Tommy Webster was the coach for a while. And then Phil Esposito coached and became GM. And then Michel Bergeron came in and replaced Phil behind the bench.

"The next season, my first full one with New York, I scored 31 goals and that was fine, and then they made the changes behind the bench and everything, and the following year they brought Guy Lafleur in after he'd been retired for four years. The season begins and everything is fine, but slowly my ice time begins to disappear. Then one night Bergeron calls me in and tells me I'm not dressing. We were in St. Louis."

Dionne could see the writing on the wall. He went to see Bergeron.

"I know it's over," Dionne remembered saying to Bergeron. "So why don't we handle this like men and make a deal right now? Bergeron didn't like what I was saying and he said something, so I said, "Look, you're not my boss, you're just the coach. Let's get Phil in and get this thing figured out.'"

Dionne had another year left on his contract. The Rangers were not prepared to just let him go and allow him to collect the rest of the money for not playing, so the team decided to send the future Hall of Famer to their farm team in Denver of the International Hockey League. The demotion was a huge blow to Dionne and his family and another example of the glaring lack of respect someone of his abilities received his entire NHL career. They'd never even think of sending someone like Lafleur to the minors. That would have been the ultimate insult and something that would have been condemned by the entire hockey world. But somehow it was okay to send Marcel Dionne to ride the buses again.

More than anything, it made Dionne hate Michel Bergeron. Even to this day.

"When I returned from the minors it was clear Bergeron was uncomfortable with me around," Dionne said. "He just hated it. Espo told me that he and I had to work out our differences, so I went to see Bergeron and I told him, 'Look, all you have to say to the press is Marcel is back, he might play or he might not.' But Michel couldn't bring himself to say that. It was bizarre. He knew that I knew him and what made him tick. He didn't want me around because of that. He was a phony. He was a paper tiger. Then he changed again and tried to gain my confidence and asked me to have coffee, and then he'd brag to me about what he did to Peter Stastny and some others in Quebec. All I could think to myself was: are you crazy, man?

"I ran into Bergeron years later and he wanted to talk to me. He wanted to see if we could resolve our differences. It was a joke. He told me he'd had a heart attack and was recovering, but then he said that he ran into one of his former players who told him he wished he'd died. Bergeron said to the guy, 'You hate me that much?' And the guy said, 'Yeah, I hate you that much.' And I think he woke up and realized after that he'd hurt a lot of people he coached."

The following year, Dionne showed up for Rangers training camp. His career was barely breathing, but because he was under contract he was obligated to show up if he wanted to be paid. Roger Neilson had assumed coaching duties, and it would be his job to tell Dionne it was all over.

"He called me into this room and told me there was no room for me," Dionne recalled. "He said: 'I would hate to be the guy who cuts you.' But I'd had a good camp and was having fun, so I wasn't going to make it easier and just walk away from my contract. As it turned out, Neil Smith, who was the new GM, called me to tell me I'd been released. And that was it. The next day I was already working."

Dionne was not the type to sit on his ass and cry about his lot in life. Complain occasionally, yes. But fall into a deep, dark depression about it, no. His first job out of hockey was running a little dry-cleaning store near his home in Bedford Hills, New York. He wanted to know if he had what it took to deal with the public. He wanted to know if he could put in long hours and get by on two weeks' holiday a year. Eventually, Dionne branched into other areas. He was in the plumbing business for a while, and then in real estate and then the development business. He didn't take a day off for a long time.

These days, Dionne runs a sports marketing company with one of his daughters. He sells NHL memorabilia as part of it, so the more he gets his name out there, the more contact he makes with former NHL players, the better for business. And that is why Dionne was on the Oldtimers tour. It was a marketing opportunity rather than a chance to bond again with old teammates and to get to know one-time opponents. That wasn't important to Dionne. This was a business venture, and every time a Dionne item was up for auction after a game you could see his ears perk up and his attention turn to the bidding.

"You know," Dionne said as we both took the last dregs from our coffees, "the average NHL career is still only four or five years. I had eighteen seasons. It was a wonderful trip. I feel so lucky. I had a great lifestyle. Have I stayed in touch with the Triple Crown line? No. But it was a good group. We were all hard workers and true professionals. I played in an era when you'd be gone if you didn't play hard. It's no longer that way. A guy doesn't play hard, especially if he's a superstar, and he says: 'What are you going to do, trade me?' They don't care. Everyone's contract is guaranteed. You can make enough money in three years to last a lifetime.

"I couldn't handle dealing with players like that. That's why I have no interest in going into management or coaching. No bloody way. No, I don't need any more time around people like that."

We paid our bill and began walking towards the elevator. I was sure Dionne was one of the more complicated players to ever play the game. And while I could see how he could have rubbed a lot of players the wrong way, including his own teammates, there was also something refreshing about what he had to say. The difference between Dionne and hundreds of other players who spent time in the NHL was that he said publicly what others wouldn't dare to say. Even if they believed it with all their heart. Certainly, guys today weren't going to the rink every day saying: "Oh, I just love the game of hockey." Not a chance. Some were probably going to the rink feeling overwhelming dread, although they'd never admit it.

And likely there were hundreds of players who probably felt, like Dionne, what they might have accomplished in the NHL if they'd only had better wingers, or a better centreman, or better defencemen. But not many would have the balls to say that publicly. Some things are better left unsaid, but you had to admire Dionne's honesty. Sure, he didn't have the warmest personality and he wasn't the easiest person to strike up a conversation with. And maybe he carried a grudge too openly. But at the same time there was no denying his place in the game, his 731 goals and 1,040 assists, which for years ranked him behind only Gretzky and Gordie Howe for most points in the NHL. There was little doubt that he was a legitimate legend.

A few hours later we were on the bus heading for Skyreach Place, the biggest building we had played in so far. Once we arrived at the arena, the power of Bobby Hull was immediately evident. It was amazing, the stir he created wherever he went, especially among women. Young and old. He had this great big smile and a voice that sounded like it been dragged through a tonne of gravel.

The game went like most others. We had heard the teams in B.C.'s Interior might offer a stiffer challenge, but this didn't appear to be the case. The mood in the dressing room between periods was a little muted, compared with the levity that was so common up north. But I figured it would take a couple of games for the guys to feel completely at ease with one another, and one night on the town would likely be enough to loosen everyone up.

The newcomers made an immediate impact. Tony Tanti scored twice, while Kurtenbach, Lidster and Butcher all got goals as well. Marcel and Tiger seemed to have some extra jump. Maybe it was playing in such a beautiful new arena, in front of the biggest crowd of the tour so far, but both players put on a show, with Dionne in particular making some no-look passes that drew approving shouts from the spectactors.

That night we went to a country bar called the O.K. Corral, but the guys felt the crowd was a little old for their liking. We headed over to a place called Flashbacks, which was definitely younger, which made us all feel older. Still, the beer was cold and the stories were funny, and you could see how easy it was for new hockey teams to form and for old friendships to be rekindled.

After a while, Gary Nylund and I grabbed a taxi back to the hotel. We were both bagged. As we drove we talked about our new teammates and about how strange it felt.

"That's hockey," Nylund said. "One day someone is your best friend, and the next day he's traded and you're welcoming someone else who's come to take his spot. It's strange, but you quickly adjust. You have to. You have no choice."

CHAPTER 9

THE GOLDEN JET

THE PENTICTON MEMORIAL ARENA was a grand
old hockey barn, full of history. You could feel it the
second you walked through the doors.

Its most famous inhabitants over the years had been the Penticton Vees, an unlikely group of senior men's players who won
the 1955 World Hockey Championship. The arena hadn't really
changed much since those days, structurally anyway. The stands,
however, looked like they'd received a fresh coat of paint. Some
of the bench seating was fire engine red, while other sections
were royal blue. There was a lovely old press box—had to be the
original—that looked like it could hold no more than three or
four people. It, too, was wearing a new jacket of hunter green
paint. Even the aisles had been painted—rain slicker yellow.

Walking around the top level of the arena was like walking
through a museum. And, in some ways, the arena was a museum.
The B.C. Hockey Hall of Fame was located here, which, I suppose, was an odd place to locate such an institution, but in some
ways it was fitting too. The heroics of the '55 Vees formed the

centrepiece of all the memorabilia and artifacts that could be viewed in the glass cases.

They included an enlarged copy of the front page of the *Penticton Herald* from March 17, 1955. "WELCOME WORLD CHAMPS," screamed the headline. "Thousands greet Vees as title comes HOME" said the subhead. The article detailed the Vees' stunning 5–0 walloping of the Russians in the gold medal game, with goalie Ivan McLelland getting the shutout for Canada. There were pictures of the town's hockey heroes, which included the Warwick brothers—Grant, Bill and Dick.

Just down the aisle from the exhibit on the Vees was a section for Hockey Hall of Fame inductees. Among the more prominent names was John Ferguson, the kid who grew up on the east side of Vancouver and went on to become one of the NHL's toughest customers. Ferguson played eight years in Montreal, collecting 1,214 minutes in penalties. After his playing days, he went into management, most notably with the Winnipeg Jets, where he was the GM. The Courtnall brothers, Geoff and Russ, had also been recently inducted.

When you looked at their career numbers, it was certainly impressive for a couple of kids from just outside of Victoria who some said wouldn't amount to anything in the big leagues. Although Russ was fast, his critics said he was too small to survive in a big man's game. Geoff wasn't supposed to have the talent to make it, period. Russ went on to play 1,029 games and score 297 goals and 447 assists in his sixteen-year career. Geoff, who was supposed to be the grinder in the family, would get 367 goals and 432 assists in his seventeen years in the NHL, which included a Stanley Cup with the Edmonton Oilers.

The Penticton Vees were long gone, replaced by junior hockey teams. Many of the NHL's biggest names got their start in the uniform of the Penticton Knights, including Brett Hull and Paul Kariya. Hull had played here between 1982 and 1984, setting a single-season scoring record with 105 goals, a Junior A record that still stands today. Kariya captained the same team ten years later.

Penticton was also the home of the Okanagan Hockey School, one of the longest-running and most popular hockey schools anywhere in the world. And throughout the building you could find old posters advertising some of the NHL stars who would be at the school that summer, like goaltender Andy Moog, who was raised in Penticton. Glenn Anderson was always a regular at the summer camp, as was Kevin Lowe, his teammate with the Edmonton Oilers, and Ray Ferraro, who was still playing in the NHL fifteen years after the date on his poster. It was harder to find an NHL hockey player who hadn't put in some time at the school, because Penticton was one of the nicest places in Canada during the summer.

The Memorial Arena held about 2,700 people, maybe three hundred more if the fire marshall was out of town. And when the Oldtimers took to the ice later that evening, every seat in the place was taken—which really wasn't a surprise to anyone. It was a special night for Bobby Hull in particular. This is where his son had played and scored so many goals, and when it came to the Golden Brett, there wasn't a prouder father in the world.

Before the start of the game, Ron Hoggarth grabbed his cordless microphone and went to the bench to interview Hull. This would be a running routine that would always end with Hoggarth asking Hull if he planned to be behind the bench for the game. And Hull would say: "No, these guys are incorrigible and uncoachable, so I don't think I'll bother." And then he would inform the crowd that he was going to be on the main concourse signing autographs. But because of the significance of the Penticton Memorial Arena in his son's hockey development, he took a few extra minutes to talk about Brett.

"I know Brett loved it here," Hull told the crowd. "The fans here in Penticton were always great, and Brett won't ever forget that. He turned out to be a special player, and he won't forget that it all started here."

There was, of course, big applause.

After the game got underway, Hull made his way to the building's main concourse, where a table had been set up for him. On another table close by was a stack of eight-by-ten pictures of Hull from his days with the Chicago Blackhawks that were being sold for ten dollars each. The idea was for people to buy one of the pictures and then get Bobby Hull to autograph it. Hull would get the lion's share of whatever number of pictures sold. That's not to say he refused to sign other things, like programs. But you could tell he didn't like it when some kid turned up with some scrap of paper he wanted signed.

"You'll lose that before you leave the building," Hull told one kid.

Of course, the young boys hanging around Hull knew him as the father of Brett and not as someone who was a legitimate NHL superstar in his own right. The kids had to rely on their parents to fill them in on whose autograph they were actually getting. Still, it didn't stop kids from asking him if he was "Brett Hull's dad."

"Yes, I am," Hull told one blond-haired youngster.

"Can you sign his autograph for me?" the boy replied.

Hull was not beyond setting kids straight about manners. When one boy asked Hull for an autograph without saying please, he looked at him sternly and said: "You mean, can I have an autograph please, don't you?" He wasn't shy about voicing his opinions on things, especially when it came to Brett and his coaches. Bobby Hull never made a secret of his dislike for Brett's former coach in Dallas, Ken Hitchcock. Brett made no secret of it either, when he played with the Stars. Father and son were both happy when, in the off-season, Brett signed a deal with the Detroit Red Wings.

"Too bad Brett had to leave Dallas," one youngster said to Hull.

"Why?" Bobby replied. "So he could stay and play for that tub of guts (Hitchcock)?"

The comment didn't even register with the boy, who was all of nine or ten. But you could tell it was a line that Hull had used often. You could only imagine the joy he must have felt when he learned that Hitchcock had been fired by Dallas, even though it was certain he'd land with another NHL team by the following season.

Back on the ice, meantime, it was another blowout for the Oldtimers. It was a surprise to most of the players, who thought Penticton would ice a competitive team—maybe not one that had any chance of knocking off the former NHL players, but certainly a team that would at least make them break a sweat. But after the first period the score was 8–0, and the guys put it in cruise control the rest of the way.

After the game, we hopped on the bus for the five-minute ride to a local bar called the Barley Mill Brew Pub. It was owned by Larry Lund, a local businessman who had once played in the old World Hockey Association, or WHA. He was mostly known, however, as the person behind the famous Okanagan Hockey School.

The pub was packed when we arrived, and heads began turning as soon as the players walked through the door. There was a section that had been roped off for us, and within minutes a couple of waitresses were bringing beer and wine to the table and taking food orders. It was a great atmosphere, and the guys were really starting to bond with one another after a slow start.

Lund took over a microphone that appeared out of nowhere and gave a nice speech about the players and how nice it was to see them back in Penticton. He then began calling the players up, one at a time, to present them each with a bottle of Okanagan wine. Some guys grabbed the microphone and said a few words, like Tiger, who you knew was going to say something about the rather weak RCMP team the Oldtimers had faced-off against earlier in the evening.

"The RCMP used to hire guys who knew how to play hockey," Williams told the hockey fans who had jammed the Barley Mill. "Obviously, that's no longer the case." Everyone laughed. "We don't mind kicking your ass," Williams continued. "We'd just like to break a sweat doing it."

Soon Lund was introducing Bobby Hull, who got a loud ovation from everyone, like he always did. Before giving the floor to Hull, Lund told the crowd that he owed the former Blackhawk a lot. He said that Hull's move to the WHA helped raise salaries everywhere in the game and that a lot of people, including himself, had cashed in on the back of Hull's controversial move.

"I was making $22,000 a year in the minors," Lund told the crowd. "I got paid $150,000 a year when I got a job in the WHA with the Houston Aeros. Sometimes people forget that what Bobby did paved the way for a lot of us to make a pretty decent living for a while, and I just wanted to say thanks all these years later."

Everyone started clapping, and then Hull took over. Like his son, Brett, there wasn't a mike Bobby didn't love. Sometimes, however, Bobby and mikes could be a dangerous mix. You were never quite sure what was going to come out of Bobby's mouth. You hoped it was clean and suitable for family listening, but you were never sure.

Many years ago, Hull had had an ugly divorce from his first wife, Joanne, mother of the four Hull boys. Years later, Hull never passed up an opportunity to take a shot at her. Even in public.

"People have asked me what I'd do if I learned I only had two weeks to live," Hull told the crowd. "I tell them I'd ask to be with Brett's mother, because it would seem like an eternity."

Some of the audience in the Barley Mill laughed, but just as many moaned. Bobby, he just smiled. Then he started in on another story about the day he and his current wife were walking in a field and came across a bull and three heifers.

"The bull goes up to the first heifer, sniffs her and then breeds her," Hull continued.

"Then the bull goes up to the second heifer, takes a sniff, and then mounts her and breeds her. Then he does the same thing to the third heifer that's there. My wife is just standing there in amazement. 'Did you see that?' she says to me. 'Why can't you do that?' I said to her: 'Honey, you get me three different females and I'll do it, believe me.'"

Most of the guys just shook their heads, trying to cover the smiles on their faces. That was Bobby, classic Bobby. Somehow, it didn't seem to diminish him in any way in the eyes of the crowd. Most of the people, in fact, ate it up. Hull was a cowboy who didn't really care what you thought of him. He was who he was, and certainly wasn't going to change at age sixty-three.

Hull and I had shared a coffee earlier in the day. He loved talking about hockey, and I imagined he probably had five million stories locked away in that head of his. No one told a story quite like Hull, and the truth was he'd been collecting them from the time he was a little kid. He had a wonderful way with language that sometimes made you laugh. He liked to say that when he was a little boy, he had so much energy he was "on a dogtrot everywhere I went." A hockey puck was always "the biscuit." Someone he knew was "no bigger than a minute." Women were "doll" or "sweetheart" or "gorgeous." Which maybe didn't make you laugh, but it did make you marvel at the fact that he got away with it so easily in this day and age. Far from being offended, however, the women he came across seemed to enjoy Hull's flirtatious nature. Or at least tolerate it without protest.

If Hull had an edge, if it seemed all his humour was locker-room humour, it was easy to understand why. Hull had grown up near Belleville, Ontario, a hockey prodigy who left home at fourteen to begin his junior hockey career. Four years later he was playing for the Chicago Blackhawks in the NHL, a place he was destined to be seemingly from birth.

Hull told me that when he was a little boy his family had an old Philco radio that didn't have any kind of antennae, so reception of any sort was dicey. But on Saturday nights he would turn the radio on and listen to Foster Hewitt call Leafs games and pray that the reception held when the games got exciting. Often it didn't, but Hull hung in there until it returned and would go to sleep at night with Hewitt's play-by-play ringing in his head.

The NHL that Hull joined was a far cry from the league that exists today. At that time, in a league with only six teams and 120 players, many fans knew every player on every team. There were no names sewn on the backs of their jerseys then, but it didn't matter, said Hull. Fans could see the players' faces, could tell who they were by the way they skated, by the way they shot the puck, by the way they threw punches.

"People could relate to us," Hull said, pushing aside his coffee cup. "We were real to the fans. They could touch us. We signed autographs before the game, reaching over the glass. And the other thing is, we entertained them royally and we knew the fans would keep coming back if we continued to entertain them. Why do you think they still come out to see us? Because we damn well entertained them. The other thing is people didn't see us as rich, spoiled athletes. We made a tuppence."

Hull had a thing about helmets. He believed, like many of the game's oldtimers, that the game changed the day helmets were introduced into the NHL. That players no longer worried about carrying their sticks high or hitting opponents in the head, because the guy had a helmet on. And what happened, Hull said, was players eventually lost respect for one another.

It wasn't a new theory, and it completely ignored the new

realities of the game. Players were bigger, faster, stronger. Concussions from body checks were never more numerous. If anything, helmets didn't offer enough protection, given the new dynamics of the modern game. But Hull's stand on helmets and what they had done to the game was a comment on the state of the hockey as a whole and the direction it had gone over the years. Although today's players were better trained, better conditioned and certainly better paid, the game itself was in worse shape, Hull believed.

Helmets had not only eliminated mutual respect, but worse, the game was no longer the free-flowing, end-to-end affair that it often was when Hull had roamed the ice. More often than not, any flow was being dragged down under the weight of a league full of muckers and grinders, hooking and clutching and grabbing their way to multi-million-dollar paycheques, he felt.

Hull said he first sounded the alarm about where the game was headed way back in 1969. He told the *Montreal Gazette's* legendary hockey writer, Red Fisher, that he feared the game was being taken over by "untalented goons whose only job is to go out and destroy opponents." The Golden Jet said Fisher never did anything with his stuff for several years—ten, to be precise. And then one day he saw an article of Fisher's that said almost the same thing Hull had predicted a decade earlier.

It was a drum that Hull's son Brett would eventually start beating himself, much to the chagrin of executives at NHL headquarters but to the never-ending delight of his father.

Quick lips weren't the only thing Brett Hull had in common with his famous father. Brett had the same stocky build, the same rugged features and wrists the size of cooked hams. And he used them to get a shot off as quickly as his father did, according to Bobby.

"When Brett was a little boy," Hull said in the raspy voice his son inherited from his dad, "he used to come and watch our practices. He'd watch us shoot a pail of pucks, and then I'd invite him to take some shots himself. Christ, could he shoot it! Only Anders Hedberg and I could get it away quicker than Brett, and he was only ten at the time.

"Brett even warms up the same way I did. Does the very same things. And he's a mouthpiece, too. He's now saying the same things I did forty years ago. He cares about the game the way I cared about it. He's saying they're taking the game away from the talented players, and he's right. Everyone knows he's right, and yet all he does is get grief for it. Like Ken Hitchcock. He doesn't know anything about the game. He's never played it or experienced it. How does he know how to think? He's never been there."

One of the best stories Hull told was about his jump from the NHL to the WHA in 1972. At the time it was a move that rocked the hockey establishment. The WHA was a fledgling organization that needed to hit a grand slam, one so big and towering that people would talk about it for days and weeks and months. One so monumental it could shake the foundation of professional hockey itself.

It needed a star to jump ship.

Hull was the perfect candidate. At the time there were few players in the NHL who had as much drawing power. But he was also someone who wasn't afraid to rock the boat, to do something dramatic to draw attention to himself or to a cause. Beyond that, if the WHA wanted to throw the kind of money at him they were talking about, he would have been a fool to turn it down.

It all began, Hull told me that day, over a cup of coffee at the Hotel Georgia in Vancouver. It was around Grey Cup time in 1971, and the Blackhawks were in town to play the Canucks. An old friend of Hull's named Bob Turner, who once played with Hull in Chicago, phoned up his old teammate at the Blackhawks' hotel and said he had an associate in town who wanted to meet him.

His name was Ben Hatskin.

"We went up to the suite and made small talk for a while," Hull recalled over our coffee that morning. "I liked this Hatskin guy right from the beginning. I wasn't there five minutes and he said he'd like me to go play for his WHA team in Winnipeg. They'd drawn names, if you recall, to see which NHL players they could go after, and he'd drawn mine.

"Anyway, he told me he'd give me $250,000 a year. I told him that was very nice offer, but I thought I could get that from Chicago. That was the other thing, I was negotiating with Chicago for a new contract. And while Bill Wirtz (the owner) was sailing around the Caribbean on his 110-foot ketch *The Blackhawk*, they had this little shyster lawyer trying to sign me. I told Hatskin that I still had the rest of the year left on my contract and didn't want to talk about anything until that was finished."

Hull and Hatskin shook hands, and the Blackhawks star winger figured that was the end of it.

Hatskin wasn't prepared to give up so easily and started to work different channels. For instance, he started phoning Hull's financial advisor Harvey Wineberg, trying to impress upon him how much he'd be prepared to pay his client and what it would mean to his bottom line. Meantime, negotiations with the Hawks were not going well, and Hull remembers getting increasingly frustrated.

"I'd given this team fifteen years of blood, sweat and tears, and this little prick lawyer was just browning me off," Hull recalled.

Hatskin, meantime, was ratcheting up the pressure. It got to the point that Hull instructed his accountant to tell them to get lost. But Hatskin wanted to know what it would take to get their star player.

"Harvey said to me, 'Just give me something.' I said, 'Okay.' I figured I could play another five years. I believed I could get $250,000 a year in Chicago. So I said, 'If they want to pay me that and then add a million, they've got themselves a hockey player ha, ha, ha.' I would have been the first million-dollar player ever, and so I thought that would be the end of it."

Wineberg went back to Hatskin with the player's demand. Hatskin didn't flinch and told Hull's money-man to tell his client not to do a thing with the Hawks. There were other teams in the WHA, and negotiations immediately began to get all the teams to help share the costs of the one-million-dollar bonus the league was going to have to come up with to land Hull. Hatskin figured Hull's presence in the league would give it instant credibility, something that would benefit every team—so every team should help bear some of the burden of luring him from the NHL.

Besides, Hatskin argued, Hull would fill their rink every time he was in town. And he could make all sorts of promotional appearances on the league's behalf. It wasn't the easiest sell of Ben Hatskin's life, but it wasn't the hardest, either. As negotiations among the WHA owners continued, Hatskin would update Wineberg on the progress of talks.

"I just never imagined in a million years they'd come up with the loot," Hull continued. "But then I'd get a call from my guy and he'd say, 'Just talked to Hatskin, they've got $500,000.' And then a few days later he called and said, 'Now they have $750,000.' At that point I knew I was gone. Ben Hatskin was going to find another quarter million no problem, and then, sure enough, he called one day and said he'd found the money. He had the million. Well, I was screwed then. I had given my word. I couldn't renege on the deal. I thought, 'I'm going to Winnipeg. I've got to go to goddamn Winnipeg.'"

Hull was in Red Deer, Alberta, doing some promotional work for Ford, when the story broke that the Winnipeg Jets had reached a deal with Hull that would bring him to the World Hockey Association. Bill Wirtz's son Arthur had a five-year contract with $1.25 million delivered to Hull almost immediately. By then, it was too late.

"I told Arthur to take the contract and tell Mr. Wirtz to shove it where the sun don't shine," Hull recalled.

When he realized he was losing his biggest star, Wirtz went into full damage control. He told reporters Hull was trying to hold the Hawks to a one-million-dollar ransom. "That was bullshit. All I said to the Hawks at the time was that I wanted a five-year contract. They got the one million dollars after it was revealed that I was going to get a million up front from the WHA and $250,000 a year as long as I wanted to play. That's where the million dollars came from."

While the money was nice, Hull said, he cringed at the implications of the move.

"I had an extravagant wife and five kids," Hull said. "I thought, 'Oh, shit. I'm going to have to lug them across the country and we'd just moved into a new home in Chicago.' I thought, 'Knowing my wife, this is going to be a bloody fiasco.' I also thought the Blackhawks, knowing them, would try and sue me for what I was doing and try and make me a scapegoat in the whole thing."

Sure enough, the whole affair went to court and ended up before a district judge, Hull recalled. "I was lucky there because he ruled that nobody owns nobody. Just because a team signed you to one contract, it didn't mean they had your services in perpetuity."

Hull's father had warned him that what he was about to embark on would not be easy. There would be some public backlash, for starters. But also, carrying an entire hockey league on his back would be a grind.

"I remember saying to Dad: 'Tough? What do you mean, it's going to be tough? I'm only thirty-two. I've got another five years in me. What are you talking about?' Well let me tell you it *was* tough. He was right. I lost a bunch of weight. I never ate with the team, because I was always flying into towns ahead of time to do promotional stuff like talking to the junior chamber of commerce. That was part of the deal."

Still, the hardest blow to result from his decision was delivered early on. In 1972, NHL player agent and hockey czar Alan Eagleson had arranged an eight-game series of the league's best players against the Soviet Union's best players. Ever since he first got wind of it, Hull was looking forward to being part of the encounter. But when his move to the WHA was confirmed, Hull was no longer included in the Team Canada roster.

"If there was any disappointment in my twenty-three-year career, that was it," Hull said. "That one really hurt. Apparently, I wasn't Canadian anymore. If I hadn't had so much on my plate at the time I would have taken those pricks to task over that, let me tell you." But he didn't, and instead he had to watch the series unfold on television, like the rest of us. Hull remembered watching the first game of the series in Montreal. He saw Canada score the first two goals like everyone else, but he saw something else, too. Something that held a clue to the outcome.

"The cameras panned the Canadian bench in the first period, and sweat was just rolling off the faces of the guys," Hull said, thinking back to a fall day thirty years earlier. "Then they panned the Russian bench, and they hadn't even broken a sweat yet. I said: 'Oh, oh. This isn't over yet.'"

He was right. The Soviets went on to win Game 1 of the series that went on to become an epic war between the two countries. Hull would have his own chance to play the Soviets two years later, when the WHA put together its own All-Star team for a showdown. He became the highest-scoring North American hockey player ever against the famed Russian goaltender Vladislav Tretiak.

"I scored two on him the first game, in Quebec City," Hull remembered. "He and I were the last two guys to shake hands, and I remember him saying to me: 'Bobby, how do you do that?' Hull scored three on Tretiak in the fourth game, in Vancouver, and another three later, in Winnipeg. The series would be one of the highlights of Hull's remarkable career.

After sitting out a month because of the Blackhawks' court case against him, Hull went on to score 51 goals and add 52 assists in 63 games in his first year in the WHA. His best of six seasons in the league was 1974–75, when he scored an amazing 77 goals.

Never one to shy away from controversy, Hull staged a one-man, one-game strike to protest violence in hockey during the 1977–78 season, an issue he still cares passionately about today. Too many goons in the NHL, he still says, not enough guys who can skate and shoot. He retired after playing only four games that season but made a return the following year, when the NHL accepted four WHA teams into its league—including the Jets.

His body, however, couldn't take it. He was injured almost from the start and ended up playing only twenty-seven games for Winnipeg and Hartford, where he only scored six times. He retired for good that year and ended up finishing his NHL career with 610 goals and 1,170 points in 1,063 games. He was inducted into the Hockey Hall of Fame in 1983.

What was it about Hull that people seemed to love so much? First, they loved the way he played—full-throttle, fearless with a shot as powerful as a bazooka. They loved his charm, too, especially the women. Hey, he had it. There was a charisma about the guy that couldn't be denied. It was in his smile. In his handshake. It was in the way he skated down the wing at Chicago Stadium. And people also loved it that he spoke his mind. Rightly or wrongly, he took a stand on issues most players wanted no part of because it wasn't worth the bother.

Still, Hull wasn't without his warts. Some players felt he loved the spotlight a little too much. And much like the situation today with his son Brett, players felt Hull's criticism of the NHL and the direction the game was going was a little hypocritical. The old "bite the hand that feeds you" routine.

But there was no denying Hull's impact on the game. As a player, he was one of the modern power forwards. A five-foot ten-inch, 195-pound package of pure dynamite. But he was also a pioneer, who ended up blazing a trail that thousands of hockey players have travelled down and benefited from since. As Larry Lund said that night at the Barley Mill, if it wasn't for Hull, Lund wouldn't have made the money he did in the WHA. Hull's move also helped to shake more money out of NHL owners for players threatening to bolt to the new league too, unless their team upped the ante.

Despite everything he had done for so many, only one other person had ever thanked Hull for blazing that trail, taking the lumps and suffering the scratches that went along with it.

A few years after retiring, Hull found himself back in Vancouver to do a commercial for The Bay. He was staying at The Ritz. The Boston Bruins were in town to play the Canucks, and Hull was trying to hunt down some game tickets for friends. He was in the lobby of the hotel, talking to some players, when Wayne Cashman walked in. Cashman wasn't in the lineup that night.

"Anyway," Hull said that morning, "I introduced Wayne to my friend and said he was looking for a couple of tickets. Cashman reached in his pocket and took out four tickets and handed them to my friend. I said, 'What do I owe you for those?' He said, 'Owe me? What do you owe me? It's more like what do I owe you? You helped make me rich.' But that was it. Cashman was the only person who ever said thanks."

Just then our waitress returned to our table with her hands behind her back.

"Bobby," she said. "Would you mind signing this for a friend? I promise I won't bother you again."

"Bother me," Hull grinned. "You're not bothering me. What's your friend's name?"

"Heather."

"Is she good looking?"

And then he laughed that Bobby Hull laugh.

Back at the Barley Mill, meanwhile, the nightly auction of NHL memorabilia had begun. Most of the big names on the tour, guys like Dionne and Williams and Hull, and on the trip up north, Johnny Bower and Russ Courtnall, had sweaters with their names on the back, which were sold. They would get a cut of whatever the final price was. Lesser names like Doug Bodger and Bob Rouse and Wayne Babych had nothing.

Babych decided to do something about it.

Earlier in the day, Babych had visited a friend at a local sporting goods store and bought a St. Louis Blues jersey from him for thirty dollars. He thought he'd autograph it and put it in the auction himself, to see what he could get. Well, now the Babych jersey was on the block and the auctioneer decided to start the bidding at one hundred dollars.

You could have heard a coin drop in the place.

"Come on, folks," the auctioneer urged the crowd. "Wayne Babych once scored fifty-four goals in the NHL. He was a legend in the city of St. Louis and still is. Who will give me one hundred dollars to start?"

Not a peep.

Some of the guys had moved from the cordoned-off area, where we had been sitting for dinner, to take up spots near the bar. That way they could get a better view of the bidding action. Needless to say, the guys were enjoying seeing Babych squirm while the auctioneer tried valiantly to move the jersey he had purchased earlier in the day. You could see Doug Lidster and Tony Tanti and a few others conspiring behind the backs of their hands.

"I'll give you four dollars!" Lidster screamed out.

Everyone started laughing, including Babych.

"Okay," the auctioneer said. "I've got four dollars. Who will give me five?"

"Five," said Tony Tanti.

Tiger got the bidding up to twenty dollars and then came over and asked everyone if they'd be willing to throw in ten dollars to get the bid over a hundred. After much grumbling, everyone agreed. However, Babych would eventually be spared the embarrassment of having his signed jersey bought by his teammates. His friend who owned the sports store where he had purchased the jersey in the first place came through and paid one hundred dollars for the sweater he'd sold Babych for thirty dollars earlier in the day.

"See," Babych beamed, "that was a piece of cake. I'll have to pick up another jersey for our next stop."

"I wouldn't do that if I were you," Tiger bellowed. "We won't bail you out again."

CHAPTER 10

SURVIVOR: THE GARY NYLUND STORY

O F ALL THE FORMER NHL players who had laced
up their skates for the Oldtimers, few were as impressive as Gary Nylund. Or as funny.

Nylund's humour was hard to describe. You had to hear it. You
had to see it. When he told a story, he would often contort his
voice and scrunch up his face to make whatever he was saying
ten times as hilarious. It was not a comedic routine that translated easily to paper or the retelling, and usually when you tried
to reprise one of his stories you ended up saying: "Ahhh, you had
to be there."

And you did.

But there didn't seem to be a day that went by on the tour
when we weren't in a restaurant or bar or on the bus and there
would be a burst of noise from the guys sitting with Nylund,
whose large hands would be in full flight. Strange sounds would
be coming from his mouth, and everyone listening would be dou-
bled over in laughter.

"He's like the Pied Piper," Marcel Dionne had said one day up north, observing a group of the guys sitting around Nylund as he told another story.

But there was more to Nylund than his ability to hold a crowd. When it came to talking about life in the NHL, and life after the NHL, there wasn't a more articulate voice on the team.

After playing in Penticton, we made a short hop the next day to nearby Vernon. The small Okanagan city with a population of about twenty thousand is situated at the confluence of five valleys and bounded by three lakes—Kalamalka, Swan and Okanagan. The area is a popular tourist destination, particularly in the summer, when tours of the local wineries bring in thousands of visitors.

The Okanagan, however, is perhaps best known for a certain monster said to exist in Okanagan Lake. The native people called the creature N'xa'xa'etkw, and it was said to live in an underwater cave. The first white settlers heard of N'xa'xa'etkw from the natives. There were stories of horses swimming in the waters and suddenly being dragged beneath the surface, never to be seen again. In 1926, according to local lore, a little song was composed and sung at a banquet in Vernon. In the song, the area's infamous lake monster was referred to as Ogopogo. The name caught on and it soon became as famous as Scotland's Loch Ness monster.

"I think I just saw it!" someone at the back of the bus screamed as we drove alongside an area lake.

"No, that was just Jimmy (Mann) going for a dip," came the reply.

Vernon had a new arena that wasn't quite as grand as the one in Kelowna, but it was a good size and had bright yellow girders inside that reminded me of the rink in Nashville, Tennessee, that the NHL Predators played in. The rink in Vernon held about five thousand spectators, and we were expecting a sellout.

The bus pulled up to the rink and we dumped our equipment,

and then a few of us headed out to grab a bite to eat. We didn't have to play for five hours, so we had some time to kill and found a restaurant downtown. Nylund and I grabbed a table by ourselves. For the next hour, one of the funniest people I had ever met didn't crack a joke. But boy, did he have a story to tell.

Gary Nylund was born in Surrey, B.C., the son of an RCMP officer. When Gary was three, his father, Arnold, was transferred to the northern B.C. city of Prince George, where his son first caught the hockey bug. Once he did this, he became impervious to the bitterly cold winter nights in Prince George. When he had skates on his feet and a stick in his hand, Gary Nylund didn't know what the temperature was outside.

Growing up, Nylund was a Toronto Maple Leafs fan. Every Saturday night, like many six- and seven-year-old boys in Canada, he settled in front of the television with the rest of his family to watch *Hockey Night in Canada*. One Saturday night in 1970, the family had just finished watching the hockey game when the picture on their television set suddenly disappeared and the screen went snowy. A few minutes later, the phone rang.

Arnold Nylund answered it, and after a brief conversation he grabbed his coat and headed out into the dead-cold December night.

"I'll never forget it," Nylund said, setting down his menu for a moment. "I had never seen my dad with his gun unless he was in full uniform. But I remember seeing him strap on his gun that night, so I knew something was up."

As it turned out, the phone call that night was to inform Nylund's father that an irate man had stormed into the Prince George offices of the CBC with a gun, upset that CBC Television wasn't showing the Leafs game that night, but a regional game between the Vancouver Canucks and the California Golden Seals instead. As it turned out, the man was a gravel pit operator from nearby Fort St. James and, the world would soon learn, the father of Brian Spencer, a professional hockey player who was playing his first game of the season with the Leafs that night.

Roy Spencer had learned at noon that day that the Prince George CBC outlet, which served Fort St. James, was carrying the Vancouver–California game instead of the Toronto game. He stewed about it all afternoon. He had hoped to pick up the game on the radio but discovered he couldn't do that, either. After first phoning the station around 5 P.M. to complain, he set off on the two-hour drive to Prince George to take matters into his own hands. In his pocket he carried a 9 mm Magnum pistol.

When he arrived at the CBC station, Roy Spencer pulled his gun on an employee entering the front door and went in with him. Within minutes, he was screaming: "There is going to be a revolution across the country over the CBC!" and ordering production workers in the control room to take the station off the air. Spencer was described by CBC employees later as "cold sober but shaking like a leaf."

Spencer lined the staff of eight against a wall.

"I don't want to kill anybody. I have killed before. I killed many times in the commandos. Turn the TV off." And at 7:48 P.M. the station went off the air.

Once Spencer was convinced that the station was off the air, he backed out of the studio and ran for the front door. The station staff ran out the back door, where the police, alerted by a phone call from one of the CBC employees, were waiting. When the police were told that Spencer had gone out the front door, they ran around the building to find the armed man standing on the sidewalk.

RCMP Corporal Roger Post told Spencer to surrender and put down his gun. Spencer opened fire instead. One shot hit Post's holster. A second shot hit another officer in the foot. That's when the RCMP opened fire. Spencer was hit with three shots. Two hit him in the chest and another hit him in the face. He fell to the ground. He would be pronounced dead on arrival at Prince George Regional Hospital.

Brian Spencer was notified in Toronto of his father's death. In the game, Toronto had defeated Chicago 2–1. Spencer was interviewed by Ward Cornell between periods and before the shootings took place.

Gary Nylund remembers his dad coming home that night. He remembers his father talking to his wife, Sylvia, about what had happened and how he had pulled his gun but never fired a shot. He remembers thinking how strange it was that something like hockey could drive a person to such extremes.

"For weeks," Nylund said. "It was the story in Prince George. I thought about the whole thing a lot, even years after. I remember thinking how odd it was—Brian Spencer was just one hockey player, and this guy was the father of one hockey player playing thousands of miles away. That's when I first realized there was something to this hockey thing. The impact one player could have on a whole country. I was really tied in to the mystery of the NHL after that. The grip it has on this country. The strange power it has over people. I'm not sure the players think that way anymore, but I certainly did."

"The shooting made you realize how big a deal hockey was in Canada?" I asked.

"Absolutely," Nylund continued. "And time is a very strange thing to me now. Time crawled along when I was playing hockey. It didn't go very quickly until it was over, and then you say to yourself, where did it go? Where did that eleven years go that I played in the league? You know, I was eighteen and then I was twenty-nine. What happened? Then your kids are born and before you know it, they're eight years old. Time is a very strange thing in the NHL because it goes so fast. I still think about that night the whole Spencer thing happened because it was the start of something for me. It was an awakening. The fact that the

Leafs were involved and they were my team, and that I would go on to play for the Leafs, it was all so strange. There was this whole connection between the night in my living room when it happened and the day I walked into Maple Leaf Gardens for the first time. I get chills thinking about it sometimes."

The Nylunds relocated to the Vancouver area a few years after the shooting. Gary became one of the top minor hockey players in the area, starring in the North Delta Minor Hockey system and eventually in the Western Hockey League with the Portland Winterhawks. Nylund was big, six feet four inches, and mean and could skate as well as most forwards. He was Chris Pronger before Chris Pronger was invented. He helped Canada win a gold medal at the World Junior Championships, and when he became eligible to be drafted by the NHL he was a consensus top-three pick.

"There were three of us that year (1982) who were projected to go top three: Gord Kluzak, Brian Bellows and myself," Nylund now recalled, nearly twenty years later. "Boston had the first pick, Minnesota had the second, Toronto had the third and Philadelphia had the fourth pick. The day before the draft, which was held in Montreal that year, I had interviews with the top teams. My agent and I met with Harry Sinden, and he said Boston was either going to take Kluzak or myself. They liked Kluzak's offensive abilities, and they liked me more defensively. Then we talked to Minnesota and they said they needed a forward and would take Bellows if he was available, and if he wasn't they were going to take me or Kluzak."

They were meeting with Toronto's GM, Gerry McNamara, next.

"Now, you can imagine with me being a Leafs fans all my life, I really wanted to play for the Leafs. And we're just about to go into the meeting when my agent, Norm Caplan, says to me: 'Now, when you go in there I want you to say you won't play for them.' And I'm like: 'What? Why?' Well, he felt Toronto had a horseshit team and would have for years, and if I didn't go one or two I'd be better off with Philadelphia, which had the makings of a good team. So he's like: 'Got it? Just tell him you won't play for his team because you don't think they're going to be very competitive and you want to play for a team that has a chance to go places.'"

Nylund couldn't believe what he was hearing. The Leafs were his team. When he was a kid, he was every great Leaf who ever played. This was the opportunity millions of Canadian boys dreamed of while growing up, and he was being told to kiss it goodbye. Before Gary Nylund knew it, he was sitting in front of Gerry McNamara, mumbling like a ten-year-old.

"Ah, I don't want to play for the Leafs," Nylund said, in a performance as unconvincing as any he would ever give in his life. "I don't think you're going to be very competitive, and I'd . . ."

Nylund didn't get a chance to finish. McNamara didn't care what the young player in front of him thought. If Nylund was still available at Number 3 he would be taken by the Leafs. Period.

And he was.

Gary Nylund would never forget arriving at Maple Leaf Gardens for the first time to be introduced to the local media. Every step he took in the old building was like flipping a page in a history book. The walls were covered with pictures that chronicled so many of the great moments that had occurred in the building. "Oh my God," Nylund remembered thinking. "I'm here. I've made it. This was the team I watched on television every Saturday night. This was the only team I ever wanted to play for. I'm a Leaf. I'm a Leaf!"

But a few months later, when he showed up for his first training camp, Nylund realized the Leafs team he was joining bore little resemblance to the teams whose great achievements were frozen in time on the Gardens' walls. Where was Johnny Bower? Where was Darryl Sittler? Where was George Armstrong? Who were these guys on the ice wearing Leafs socks and Leafs sweaters? These were the guys now carrying the torch? The guys being asked to carry on the tradition of one of the greatest sports franchises in the world?

As it turned out, Nylund's timing couldn't have been worse. He had arrived to be part of one of the sorriest chapters in the team's illustrious history. By the early 1980s, Harold Ballard's reign as owner was reaching its nadir. Ballard had become synonymous with the sad deterioration of the once-proud organization. The front office was a mess. On the ice, the team was horrible. There was little talent and even less leadership. Players couldn't stand coaches, and coaches couldn't stand players.

It was out of control.

Nylund roomed with the famed Leafs defenceman Borje Salming. As fans would learn years later, Salming was one of the thirstier members of the Leafs teams during that era. He partied hard, and his world eventually included drugs too. Nylund, of course, knew none of this when he joined the team. All he knew was what he saw on television whenever he watched the Leafs— an all-star defenceman who was as talented and tough as they came. But early on in his rookie season, Nylund learned that Salming didn't like to get to bed too early. In fact, he would usually stroll back to the team's hotel when the Leafs were on the road in the early morning hours, and even then he wasn't ready to hit the sack.

"He'd come in and turn the television on," Nylund remembered. "I don't know how he did it. But when I was a rookie I didn't open my mouth. I'd lie there, listening to the TV, and I'd be so mad because I couldn't get to sleep, but I didn't say anything. The second year I felt different, and one night he came in and it was like three or four in the morning and he turns the TV on. Well, I'm not playing well at the time, and I figure to hell with this. I need my sleep so I'm going to say something. "Borje, turn that damn TV off. I can't get to sleep and it's screwing up my play. So turn the goddamn thing off."

Salming still couldn't turn it off. Instead, he went and sat in front of the TV with his back against his bed and his knees up. He turned the sound down so low that he could barely hear it and had to strain to catch the words.

"I remember thinking to myself," Nylund would recall that day in the restaurant. "Look at the guy. This is one of the greatest defencemen to ever play the game, and he's sitting in front of the TV, all hunched over, trying to hear the words. It was kind of pathetic and yet it was amazing, too, given what this guy could do on the ice every night. You never would have guessed he was like this away from the ice. But I always wondered what he would have been like had he taken care of himself. He was an amazing guy and a really great guy too."

In the last exhibition game in his first season with the Leafs, Nylund ended up in a collision with Wilf Paiement of the Quebec Nordiques. Somehow, his knee ended up snapping backwards, officially known as a "hyperextension." According to team doctors, it would be five or six months before Nylund was back on the ice again.

Nylund ended up returning after ninety days, a recovery described by some as miraculous. It was a medical marvel unprecedented enough to be written up in a medical journal. Little did anyone know that his miracle recovery was actually a mirage.

Nylund returned just after Christmas and had played eight games when he was skating off the ice at the end of a shift and bumped into linesman John Dimico. It was an innocent-looking collision that would have serious consequences. Nylund injured the same knee, but this time it was the anterior cruciate ligament. The knee, as it turned out, wasn't as strong as most had thought, and Nylund's first season in the NHL was finished. And most of his second one, too.

"I remember going to see the doctor at the time of the second injury," Nylund remembered. "And he told me that he could get me four more years out of that knee. I ended up getting another nine, so that was pretty good. And all the other knee injuries I had in the NHL were cartilage problems. But it was after the second one that I really changed my outlook on the NHL. Playing became all about survival. I didn't want to be one of those guys who played a few seasons and then it was over. I remember thinking that ten years was a good amount of time to play. It was respectable. And when I'd go out on the ice sometimes, standing for the national anthem, I would write the number ten on the ice with my stick. It was just to remind myself what the goal was."

After his fourth season with the Leafs, a little-known clause in the NHL Players' Association contract with owners allowed Nylund to become a restricted free agent. He was only twenty-two years old at the time and had already played four years in the league. Still, no one in Toronto thought that Nylund would actually go anywhere. What young player would want to leave the Leafs, regardless of how poor they were?

Well, Gary Nylund, as it turned out.

He'd had enough of Toronto. He didn't think the team was going anywhere, and his time there mostly stirred up lousy memories. If there was an opportunity to move on, why not take it? His agent, Roland Thompson, began negotiations with the Chicago Blackhawks, an Original Six team that looked like it was building towards a bright future. Even a Stanley Cup. The summer after his fourth year in Toronto, Nylund and his agent reached a tentative deal with the Hawks' GM, Bob Pulford.

"So, we decided we're going to play for Chicago," Nylund said that day as our chicken salad sandwiches arrived. "They tell us to fly to Chicago and go to the main airport hotel. There would be someone to meet us in the lobby who would escort us up to a room, and then we'd come back down, get back on a plane and fly back to Vancouver, where we were to keep our mouths shut.

"Pulford wanted to sign the contract on Chicago soil, for some reason. Anyway, we agree to this and land in Chicago, and as we're walking through the concourse of the airport Rollie is paged. He goes to the nearest phone, and it's Glen Sather (GM of the Edmonton Oilers at the time). Sather says, 'I know you're there to sign with the Blackhawks. I know all about it.' He wants me to play for them. He says he can't give me as much as Chicago and he can't give me more than Randy Gregg, an Oiler defenceman, because the Oilers just won a Stanley Cup. Anyway, to make a long story short, Rollie and I look at one another and decide we're signing with Chicago. I was way ahead financially with Chicago, and we told Sather that. He says: 'But we're going to win at least three more Stanley Cups,' which they did. And if I have a regret about my career, that's probably the number one regret I have. That I took the money instead of the best opportunity to win a Cup."

After hanging up on Sather, Nylund and his agent continued on to the airport hotel to meet Pulford. They sorted out a few details, and then the big defenceman signed on the dotted line. Nylund would never forget Pulford's next words to him.

"Okay," Pulford told him. "As of this moment you are a Chicago Blackhawk, but you are not to tell anyone. When you go home, I want you to continue to negotiate with Toronto. Let the chips fall where they may, and then I'll enter the picture."

Pulford didn't want Nylund to say anything to the Leafs because there was still the matter of compensation to iron out. For signing Nylund, the Blackhawks were going to have to give something up. Given that Nylund had been a high first-round draft pick and was rounding into a solid NHL defenceman, the Blackhawks were likely going to have to give up a quality player or two to the Leafs in exchange. But in his concurrent negotiations with the Leafs, McNamara was trying to use Nylund's knee injuries against him. Pulford thought if McNamara went public with those concerns it would help reduce the amount of compensation Chicago would have to offer in exchange for a hobbled blue-liner with only one good leg.

The deal with the Blackhawks was eventually made public in August 1986. The Leafs were not amused. Nylund would have three solid but not spectacular seasons with the Blackhawks, beset by more injuries. In November 1988, he was packaged with Marc Bergevin and sent to the New York Islanders in exchange for Steve Konroyd and Bob Bassen.

Nylund's final NHL game would arrive during the 1992–93 season in a game against the Calgary Flames. Nylund was going into the corner to hit the Flames' Sergei Makarov, who saw the Islanders defenceman at the last minute and ducked down to avoid getting creamed. Nylund's knee ended up getting the worst of it, and he knew instantly it was bad.

"I knew it was the anterior cruciate again," Nylund recalled of that day. "So I started processing the whole thing right there on the ice. Okay, I've been through this before. I know it's going to be ten months because it heals ten per cent each month. And I'm thinking, 'No, that's it. I can't go through this anymore. I can't.' And I remember Uwe Krupp was my teammate at the time; he was helping me off the ice and I had my arm around him and I said: 'That's it, Uwe. I'm done. This is it.'"

And it was.

Nylund went to see a doctor about his knee. He was told it could be reconstructed again and that he could probably get another couple of years out of it, if he wanted. The doctor asked Nylund about his insurance policy and how much it paid. When Nylund told him, the doctor suggested he just take the money and retire. Nylund reacted poorly to the suggestion at first, thinking the doctor had a lot of nerve suggesting he hang up his skates.

That wasn't the way Nylund wanted his career to end. But for the first time, Nylund could see the end. He could see the other side. He was Alice peering through the looking-glass, and he wasn't sure he was ready to take that step.

"I talked to my wife about it," Nylund said as we continued to chat. "And I remember talking to my parents, and they were all for me hanging them up. They thought I'd been through enough. And so I decided that would be it, although I never made an announcement. I never did really tell anyone I was going to retire. I just sort of faded away, like an old pair of jeans. There was no closure. Even though I wasn't a superstar, I figured I'd put in enough years that the end would be more significant. It didn't happen for me, and the way it ended bothered me for a number of years."

Nylund would live with two regrets about his career. The first was that he didn't take Glen Sather up on his offer to become an Oiler. He would have had a few Stanley Cup rings if he had. The second was not getting his knee fixed the last time and giving it one more go. Even though retiring was the prudent thing to do, Nylund would live with the feeling, for a few years anyway, that he took the insurance money and ran. And consequently, that his NHL career ended with a fizzle, not a bang.

"On some level I know that the decision was probably the right one," Nylund told me that day. "But on another, I can't help but think of what I missed by not getting the knee fixed. I probably could have played three more years. That would have been three more years' worth of stories."

Perhaps because of the circumstances of his retirement, getting on with his life as Joe Citizen wasn't easy for Nylund. He and his wife, Janice, returned to Vancouver to resume their lives after hockey. After taking a few months off, Nylund worked for a landscaping company. It wasn't long, however, before he knew that wasn't going to make him happy. The thought of becoming a fireman had a certain allure. It was a demanding occupation that would probably satisfy Nylund's inherent need for an occasional adrenaline rush. But he soon discovered that in order to apply for the job he needed something he didn't have—a Grade 12 education.

Nylund went to see a favourite teacher at his old high school in North Delta. He had a proposal. He would outfit the football team in new equipment if the school would quietly graduate a student named Gary Nylund. He had something the school wanted, and the school had something he wanted. No one had to be the wiser. While it may have been tempting, the school said no to Nylund's offer, and he had no choice but to take night courses at a local college to complete his high school education. It was a humbling reintroduction to the real world, sitting there in a classroom of mostly new Canadians who barely spoke English. There he was, an athlete who had earned hundreds of thousands of dollars in the NHL, having to recite the names of the ten provincial capitals of Canada.

Nylund purchased season tickets to the Vancouver Canucks. At first, he looked forward to attending the games. He and his wife would hop in his truck and head to the game, and everything would seem fine. Then he would turn on the radio to listen to the pre-game show, and suddenly his mood would change. He would grow quiet. He'd stop talking. By the time he got to the game and saw defencemen jump over the boards that he felt weren't as good as him, even with a bad knee, Nylund would be in a foul mood.

He'd hung them up too soon, he kept saying to himself. Way, way too soon.

"WHAT WAS THE BEST part of being in the NHL?" I asked Nylund that day.

"The best part," he said, without hesitating a second, "was just being able to do the thing you do best. To do the thing you dreamed your whole life of one day doing. And that's it. There aren't many days that go by that I don't think about my playing days. It's really hard to dismiss a third of your life. It's really tough to say, 'Okay, that's over. Let's get on with the rest of my life.' I will always have that tie. I'm happy to say I had a chance to do it. I don't want to be the kind of person who hangs on to the past, but you can't dismiss it either. I will always be a part of it. I will always be part of the brotherhood. How many kids wouldn't give their left nut just to play one shift in the NHL?"

He was right. Not many. In Canada, no one had more star power than a hockey player. If you were in a bar and an NHL player walked in, the place would often go quiet. Word would spread like a brush fire.

"What was that like?" I asked Nylund.

"It's funny," he answered. "I have a cousin down in L.A. He does very well. He's a millionaire several times over. And we were sitting in his hot tub one day talking about his wants and his dreams, and he says, 'You know what my dream is? My dream is just once in my lifetime to have some kid come up and tap me on the shoulder and ask me for my autograph.' And it's true, you know, being an NHL hockey player is a status thing. I was Number 22 for the Blackhawks, and when I walked into a restaurant that's who I was. And it was always, 'It's great to have you at our restaurant.' I never stood in line for anything. And then one day it was over, and all of a sudden it was, 'Hey, buddy, back of the line.' And I wanted to say, 'Hey, don't you know who I was?'"

Another time, when Nylund was still searching for something meaningful to do with his life after hockey, an acquaintance he knew who sold for Amway came over to his house in the hopes of converting the former NHL player into a star salesman.

"So he comes over," Nylund said, putting down his coffee as he talked. "And he's driving this rusty old Datsun. We go into the living room and he pulls out all this material and puts it on the coffee table, and he's showing me this plan to sell soap and all of this other stuff. And at the end of his presentation I say, 'You know, I just don't think I'm cut out to be a salesman.' Anyway, we talk for a bit and he looks at me and says, 'Have you got a dream?' That's when I thought to myself, 'Yeah, I've got a dream, but I've already lived my dream.' The guy sat back in his chair after I said that, and he didn't have anything else to say. Then I started thinking after he left, now what am I going to do? Do I find another dream?

"It's like the Peter Brady syndrome. You know, the kid from *The Brady Bunch*. They go from these cute little kids to ugly adolescents, and nobody wants to hire them anymore. I mean, who wants Gilligan anymore? Nobody. I'm over that now, but for a while I really struggled with it. I'm sure a lot of guys do."

We paid our bill and slowly started to make our way back to the rink. Nylund eventually got his Grade 12 diploma, became a firefighter and got on with the rest of his life. And an event in the fall of 2001 allowed him finally to come to terms with the end of his NHL career.

As a one-time Leaf, Nylund had been invited back to Toronto for the official closing of Maple Leaf Gardens. Anyone who had ever donned a Leafs jersey had been invited to the splashy affair. And the night he walked onto the ice with other former Leafs was the night Gary Nylund finally let go.

"That was closure for me," Nylund said as we walked. "Because of the way my career ended, I didn't have closure. I was bitter. I was angry that I didn't play for a few more years. And I couldn't let that go. I couldn't get past how my career ended. But after the thing with Maple Leaf Gardens I found closure. I really did. I was a different person when I came home after that.

"It's funny, Tiger and I have talked about it. He felt the same way. He didn't have closure either. I know this is going to sound strange, but it's like someone dying. Your career is dead, but you never had a chance to say goodbye. So with the closing of Maple

Leaf Gardens we went back, and even though we were years removed from it, it was very important to us. They were closing that building. That meant the building was never going to be used again, and it was okay to close it."

Nylund stopped walking and turned to me.

"We were part of something that was in the past," he said, as the rink loomed in the background. "I no longer had to compare myself with anyone on the ice. It was over. It was done, and finally, I was okay with it."

That night, the Oldtimers put on quite a show. They scored three goals before the game was five minutes old. Gary Nylund was a force on the blueline, like he had been in every game he played on the tour. And whenever he wanted to, he'd wind up behind our net and take the puck the length of the ice before he'd inevitably dish it off to someone else. But despite his unselfishness, Nylund managed to score two goals.

After the game, which the Oldtimers won by thirteen goals, Nylund slowly took his equipment off and sipped on a beer. I could see scars on both his knees. I wondered if he'd still be playing in the NHL if he didn't have them.

CHAPTER 11

THE STARS COME OUT

Darryl Sittler looked ridiculous.

Ridiculously tanned, ridiculously fit, ridiculously fabulous for someone fifty-one years old. There was nothing musty about the Toronto Maple Leafs legend. On the contrary, he looked like someone who just walked off his hundred-foot yacht, a genetic lottery winner destined to make grown women melt before him and grown men slink off to seek the company of others who looked more like themselves.

Sittler had star power, and this was the star-powered Old-timers tour.

After barnstorming British Columbia's heartland, the tour stopped at a few more arenas in the north of the province and into the edges of Alberta before winding up in Lloydminster. The Old-timers usually got a competitive game on this portion of the tour from the team in Kitimat, B.C. But this time the Kitimatians were no match for the former NHLers. "We killed them," Tiger would say. "Just killed them."

A new team comprised of mostly French-speaking ex–Montreal Canadiens was then assembled for a tour of the East that started in Halifax, touched down in places like Saint John, Belleville and Kingston and ended in Ottawa. The team was changed again for a third series of games in southwestern Ontario, playing to large crowds in arenas like Copps Coliseum in Hamilton, the Memorial Auditorium in Kitchener and the Windsor Arena. I had jumped off Tiger's fall tour in Vernon to return to work and didn't play with the teams assembled for the swings through the Maritimes, Quebec and Ontario. I was waiting for the biggie.

The crowning jewel in the Oldtimers' four-series tiara was the final tour, which began in the Albertan town of Red Deer and ended ten days later at the Air Canada Centre in Toronto. This was the tour that came close to filling the 19,000-seat Pengrowth Saddledome in Calgary and the 16,000-seat Winnipeg Arena. And this was the team whose names and faces could be found on the walls of the Hockey Hall of Fame in Toronto.

Besides Sittler, the Hall of Fame legends on the team included Guy Lapointe and Steve Shutt from the Montreal Canadiens dynasty teams of the 1970s; Sittler's old linemate with the Leafs, Lanny McDonald; Buffalo Sabres superstar Gilbert Perreault, and Peter Stastny, the brilliant Slovak who played on the Quebec Nordiques with his brothers, Anton and Marian. Dale Hawerchuk, who had been inducted into the Hall just recently, was also on the team, and Bobby Hull would once again be the honorary coach and chief autograph signer. In total, this Oldtimers tour included eight former NHLers whose career achievements had earned them spots in the Hall of Fame.

It was rounded out by regulars like Mark Napier, who won Cups with the Montreal Canadiens of the 1970s and the Edmonton Oilers of the 1980s, and Andre "Moose" Dupont, who won two Cups with Philadelphia's Broad Street Bullies. Reggie Leach, who also played on one of those Cup teams with the Flyers, was in the lineup, as was Craig Muni, a defenceman who won three Stanley Cup rings with the Edmonton Oilers. Gaston Gingras, the fleet-skating blueliner who won a Cup with Montreal in 1986, was another player like Napier, Leach and Muni—not a superstar during his playing days, but a name hockey fans certainly recognized. Also in this group was Wilf Paiement, the fourteen-year NHL veteran who played nearly one thousand games in the league for seven different teams, starting with the Kansas City Scouts in 1974 and ending with the Pittsburgh Penguins in 1988.

Like any good team, there were also spots on this all-star Old-timers team for role players, the guys whose careers in the NHL were not distinguished by any particular achievement beyond making it to the big time in the first place. This group included guys like Marc Bureau, a thirty-five-year-old who had ended his career only two years earlier with Calgary; Bruce Bell, a journeyman defenceman with Quebec, St. Louis, New York and Edmonton, and Craig Levie, known to friends as Cowboy, who played a grand total of 183 games in the NHL with four different teams but was otherwise a delight to be around and good guy to have in the dressing room.

Richard Sevigny, who shared a Vézina Trophy with Denis Herron and Michel Larocque when he played with Montreal in the early 1980s, and "King" Richard Brodeur, who single-handedly led the Vancouver Canucks to the Stanley Cup finals in 1982, would split the goaltending duties.

And finally there was Jimmy Mann, the former NHL tough guy employed by the tour's promoter, Xentel DM, to make sure the buses ran on time and the equipment and players made it from one city to the next. The tour didn't work without Jimmy.

All in all, it was quite a crew. And, as I would discover, a team with that many All-Stars came with its own very distinct set of dynamics. Whether players care to admit it or not, there is a caste system on any NHL team. A team's marquee players are accorded special treatment. They often get the choice locker positions. They are most often situated among players of similar stature. Their demands, however insignificant, are instantly attended to, while the same request by a journeyman forward or defenceman might be met with a shrug and a smile.

And, in some ways, that was the way it went with retired stars, too. In the days that followed, the bigger names tended to take up seats at the back of the bus, whereas the players whose names never burned quite as brightly in the NHL firmament took up positions nearer the front. The concerns of the bigger names tended to be treated more seriously than any expressed by those who had never carried their hockey teams during their playing days. Not that the big-name stars on this team were on any grand ego trips, or expecting first-class seats on flights or people to carry their bags. And it's not like any of them went out of their way to demand special treatment. It just happened, naturally. Darryl Sittler might get a little more money to cover his costs than Bruce Bell would. Peter Stastny might get his hotel room ahead of Marc Bureau—especially if all the rooms weren't ready when we arrived.

The players flew in to Edmonton for the start of the tour. We then hopped on a bus for the ninety-minute ride to Red Deer, where we would have a few hours of downtime in our hotel before heading over to the six-thousand-seat arena, formerly known as the Centrium but now called the MX Centre. It was the home of the Western Hockey League's Red Deer Rebels, the 2001 Memorial Cup champions coached by Brent Sutter. This was a great place to start the tour because Red Deer was a hockey town, and unlike other stops, where the children in the crowd weren't quite sure who Darryl Sittler or Gilbert Perreault was or who they had played for, the NHL and its history were a part of a child's education in this prairie city.

The tour had certainly come a long way from its humble beginnings back East in the mid-1970s. Early on, Marc Verreault, the Quebec-based promoter given credit for starting the Oldtimers tour, used players as part of a travelling troupe of singers and artists who performed in small rinks throughout the Maritimes, Quebec and parts of Ontario. Originally, the players played alongside the singers in a pick-up style of game that was stopped, occasionally, for one of the singers to perform a song with the help of a small orchestra and a rudimentary sound system.

Rocket Richard was on the ice as a referee, and the players consisted entirely of ex-Habs like J.C. Tremblay, Phil Goyette, Claude Laforge and Claude Provost. The crowds were far more enamoured of the hockey game than of the singers, who were soon dropped from the card; thus the Oldtimers Hockey Challenge was born. Now, more than twenty-five years later, if the Oldtimers tour wasn't *big* business it was certainly *bigger* business.

Nearly fifteen thousand people would come out to see the team in Edmonton, and just a couple thousand fewer than that in Calgary. There would be twelve thousand at the Air Canada Centre in Toronto, and about nine thousand in Winnipeg and Vancouver. The price for a family of four was sixty dollars, which for an event like Edmonton's translated into more than $210,000. The Hockey Hall of Fame players were believed to be pulling in one thousand dollars per game to cover expenses, and the rest of the players made about half of that for each outing. There was also money being made, or at least shared, from the memorabilia auctions after the games, which were also far more profitable in the bigger centres and with the bigger names. It wasn't unheard of for an auctioneer to rake in as much as thirty grand when everything was tallied up, an amount shared between the memorabilia merchandiser, who ran both the silent and public auctions at each stop, Xentel and, of course, the player himself.

No one was getting rich from the tour, but no one seemed to be losing his shirt, either. Yes, the promoter had overhead costs, like airplanes and buses and hotel rooms, but the company also operated a pretty tight ship. A share of the gate at each city also went to a local charity. In Calgary, for instance, Xentel signed over a cheque for more than seventy thousand dollars that would be split between the Calgary Flames Foundation and the YMCA. In Edmonton, the cheque was for more than thirty thousand dollars, and in Red Deer about seven thousand. Charities also had access to all monies earned from the sale of programs (two dollars each) and any money raised from the sale of 50/50 tickets.

It was a far cry from the early days of the tour.

Steve Shutt, one of the first legitimate stars to tour regularly with the team, enjoyed telling stories about his first outings with the Oldtimers. He and his old Montreal Canadiens teammate Guy Lafleur were the main attractions, surrounded by ten or eleven players of lesser note who were looking for adventure and another road trip. Back then, Shutt said, the teams would play in front of crowds ranging from a few dozen people to several thousand. One time, the former Canadiens winger recalled, he, Lafleur and a handful of other players flew into a remote native community "way up north" at the invitation of the local Red Earth band.

"We had to fly in on those planes with skis on the bottom," Shutt said. "We get to the arena for the game and look around, and there's no one there. Not a soul in the stands. We're wondering what the hell is going on. Anyway, we look in one of the dressing rooms, and there's the other team, sitting there all dressed, with a case of beer in the middle of the floor. They paid us ten thousand dollars to come up and play them. That's all they wanted.

"So we played them and had a great time. When it was time to fly out, we went over to where the plane was. It was pitch dark, and we wondered how the hell we were going to fly out of this place. The next thing you know, all these snowmobiles start arriving and line this field with their lights. Out of nowhere, we suddenly had an airstrip and we took off. It was incredible."

Yes, the tour had come a long way since then. Now, other than the fact that they had to occasionally carry their equipment bags and the hotels weren't always five-star, the Oldtimers tour in many ways resembled the life these guys left behind in the NHL. Any travel problems that arose were generally ironed out before the players ever became aware of them. Their responsibility was to get to the bus on time; everything after that was taken care of by others.

On the bus ride to Red Deer I sat in front of Mark Napier, the ex–Montreal Canadien and Edmonton Oiler who started his career as an eighteen-year-old with the World Hockey Association in 1975. He now worked for a technology firm in his hometown of Toronto and was as nice a guy as they come.

Napier was one of those players whose NHL résumé placed him a notch down from the Hall of Famers but above the vast array of everyday veterans and journeymen whose pro careers were often indistinguishable.

After winning a Memorial Cup with the Toronto Marlboros in 1974–75, Napier was ready to turn pro. At that time, though, you had to be twenty years of age to play in the NHL, which meant that Napier had another two years to wait. His agent at the time was Gus Badali, also the agent for another highly talented junior player named John Tonelli. The WHA was interested in signing both players but was also certain that the NHL would take the players and the WHA to court if it did. Badali convinced the WHA that the NHL didn't have a leg to stand on legally if it decided to challenge the signings. So the WHA went ahead, and the NHL did indeed take them to court.

The crux of the case came down to the question: can you stop an eighteen-year-old from making a living? It took a while for the case to wind its way through the court system, but in the end the answer was no, you can't. And shortly after the decision was reached, the NHL was drafting eighteen-year-old hockey players again.

For Napier, the WHA was a wide-eyed adventure. In Toronto with the Toros, he played with such legends as Paul Henderson and Frank Mahovlich. After a year, however, the team left Toronto and relocated to Birmingham, where it became the Bulls. Pretty soon, he was living the movie *Slap Shot*.

"That was pretty wild down there," Napier said as the bus rumbled along. "I played with Dave Hanson, of the Hanson brothers in the movie. You know the story there, don't you? The movie was based on the Carlson brothers (Jack, Jeff and Steve all played in the WHA), but one of them couldn't make the filming because he was in the playoffs or something, and they couldn't change the dates because of Paul Newman's schedule, I think.

"Anyway, that's when they asked Dave 'Killer' Hanson to sub in, and to make a long story short they liked the name Hanson better than Carlson, so they changed the name of the brothers to the Hanson brothers."

Every night with the Bulls was fight night. The crowds in the American south loved the violent stuff, and the Bulls were a team that could deliver it. Napier said that one year, the team established a new record for penalty minutes by a professional hockey team in one season, shattering the previous mark by the Philadelphia Flyers by more than four hundred minutes.

Fighters on the team included Gilles "Bad News" Bilodeau, Steve "Wild Man" Durbano and Frankie "Seldom" Beaton.

"One of our guys ended up getting arrested after one game for beating a guy up with a tire iron on some trip we'd been on earlier," Napier recalled.

After three years in the WHA, Napier made the move to the

NHL. He joined the Montreal Canadiens in 1978–79, just in time for the last of the five Cups the powerful Habs would win that decade.

"It was the tail end of the dynasty," Napier remembered of joining the legendary team. "Scotty Bowman had left, and it was the first year without Yvan Cournoyer and Ken Dryden, and Jacques Lemaire wasn't around either. So three great players gone and no Scotty Bowman. But there was still enough talent on the team to win another Cup, and it was a thrill to be part of it."

While Napier was certainly aware of the history that surrounded him in the Montreal dressing room and when he walked the halls of the Montreal Forum, he wasn't awestruck in the way that some kid fresh out of junior hockey might have been. Though he was only twenty-one, he had three years of professional hockey under his shoulder pads at that point.

Although he didn't speak French, Napier did not find language to be a problem or a source of divisiveness in the Habs dressing room.

"There was some stuff written at the time about the French–English split in the dressing room," Napier said. "But I didn't see that. All the instruction was in English, and if the French guys told a joke among themselves and there were great gales of laughter, usually one of them would translate it for the rest of us.

"Naturally, the French tended to gravitate to one another and the English guys tended to hang out too. It was just easier that way. But at no time did I ever feel there was any tension in the dressing room because of the French–English thing. At least not while I was there."

Napier wore a Habs jersey for the better part of six seasons. Early in the 1983–84 campaign, he was traded to the Minnesota North Stars along with Keith Acton and a draft choice for Bobby Smith. It was a big trade at the time and a big shock for Napier, who had scored forty goals the year before in Montreal. But he wasn't in a North Stars uniform very long—ninety-seven games over two seasons—before he was on the move again.

And joining another dynasty.

"I didn't see that trade coming either," Napier said. "But I was excited when it happened. It was totally a different feeling, joining this team as opposed to the Canadiens. For starters, the Oilers were so much younger, and when I think back to the two dynasties, the two teams, it was hard to compare them really.

"Edmonton was a speed team with incredible skill. I don't think they realized how talented they really were. They could score goals with such ease that it covered up some defensive deficiencies. Montreal paid a little more attention to the defensive side of things. Guys like Bob Gainey and Doug Jarvis were defensive specialists. Edmonton had role players too, but the thing that identified that team—besides Wayne Gretzky and Mark Messier, obviously—was just the overall skill.

"After I got traded by Minnesota, in my first practice with Edmonton I was put with Messier and Glenn Anderson. It took me a while to get up to their pace and tempo, believe me. But when I did, it was sure a lot of fun. I guess when I think about the two Cups, they were both great, but I think I played more of a role with the second one than the first. But I was sure lucky to have been part of two great teams. When I look back on my career, that's something I'm certainly thankful for."

It wasn't long before we were piling off the bus and into the North Hill Inn, where Jimmy Mann stood in the lobby handing out room keys. We were soon back on the bus, however, and headed to the arena, which began filling up almost an hour before game time. Soon the lights were lowered, the strobe lights were beaming and the players were introduced as they skated onto the ice to the pulsating beat of the techno music.

Everything was the same, including Celine Dion's rendition of "God Bless America" and local figure skaters touring the ice with Canadian and American flags, which Xentel had introduced to the program in the fall as a tribute to all those who had died in the 9/11 tragedy. Back in November, when the tour began, the terrorist attacks were still fresh in people's minds and the tribute seemed fitting. Five months later, in the spring, it felt odd and uncomfortable. Even out of place. There was no mention of the calamity, like there had been in the fall, which made it seem even stranger. But soon the puck was dropped and the game was on, and the score quickly became 1–0, then 2–0, then 8–0. The NHL's version of the Globetrotters was wiping out the local version of the Washington Generals again.

It took a while for some of the guys to get going. Gilbert Perreault and Darryl Sittler both appeared a little rusty when the game began, but they got progressively better. Dale Hawerchuk, however, looked like he could still be playing in the NHL. Mark Napier still had great wheels. Steve Shutt wasn't fast anymore, but around the net there was no one better. As for me, I wasn't playing. I'd decided to take in the first three or four games from the stands and conserve my energy for when the tour headed into B.C. and a hometown crowd.

Although things appeared to be the same on the ice, between periods the dressing room looked and felt different. Maybe it was because this was the first game and the guys were still getting comfortable with one another, but as you looked around the room the French-speaking players were generally on one side and the English-speakers were scattered around the rest of the room. It could have been an accidental arrangement, but I had my doubts.

Guy Lapointe sat beside Gaston Gingras, who sat beside Moose Dupont, who sat beside Marc Bureau. Most of the time they spoke French. Across and beside them sat the others, speaking English. Not that any of this was bad, but you certainly got a feel for what it must have been like for Shutt and Napier and any other English-speaking players who were on the Canadiens during the 1970s and 1980s, when francophones dominated the lineup and the dressing room. When the same Oldtimers hopped on the bus or the plane, however, there were no cliques among the French-speaking players, and English was the universal language.

After the game we went back to the hotel, had dinner in the pub and sat through the post-game auction, which went poorly, especially considering this was Red Deer. It was the result of the confluence of three factors: bad location, too much noise, too little interest. It wouldn't be a late night.

The next morning, the guys began drifting into the hotel coffee shop shortly after 8 A.M. The bus for Calgary was leaving in an hour. A couple of us were sitting around one table when Darryl Sittler wandered in. Sittler hadn't said much in the time he had been with the team, but the guys couldn't help but notice how great he looked. Since losing his wife, Wendy, to a high-profile battle with cancer the previous summer, Sittler had spent much of his time in south Florida, where he owned one condominium and had just purchased another. The time in the sun looked good on him. There wasn't a fleck of grey on his head. He barely looked forty-one, let alone fifty-one.

He pulled up a chair, and it was soon evident that he was suffering from laryngitis or something. It was a good thing that most of us had already finished our breakfasts, because Sittler started describing how his condition had been progressively worsening and how during the night he had coughed up blood.

"You know what you do," said Ron Hoggarth, who after years on the road had picked up a trick or two. "Get some baking soda and mix it with some salt and warm water. I guarantee you it will work. I've got some baking soda back in my room."

Everyone seemed to be curious about Sittler. While he had never won a Stanley Cup during his fifteen-year NHL career, his time as captain of the Toronto Maple Leafs had conferred on him a special standing in the hockey world. And it was not like he was without his achievements. Everywhere he went, people continued to ask him about his ten-point game, that magical night he had against the Boston Bruins on February 7, 1976.

It was a story Sittler never tired of telling. There were few nights in the history of Maple Leaf Gardens as electric. Sittler would recall having seven points after two periods when the Leafs' statistician and PR guy, Stan Obodiac, came into the dressing room during the second intermission and told the team that Rocket Richard held the record for most points in a game, with eight. Sittler skated onto the ice for the third period aware of his potential to make history.

Within three or four minutes, he had tied the record. Before the game was over, he collected two more points, to set the record that still stands today. What was amazing about the night was that Sittler only had ten shots on goal the entire game, and six of them went in. The same season, Sittler would score five goals in one playoff game against the Philadelphia Flyers, which tied the NHL record. And later that summer, he would score the game-winning goal for Canada against the Czechoslvakians to win the Canada Cup.

In one season, Sittler cemented his status as an NHL legend.

While Sittler hadn't made millions during his playing days, he made enough and had invested his money wisely. Over coffee that morning in Red Deer, he told us about the new condo he had purchased near Jupiter, Florida, the huge home he had near Orillia, Ontario, and another place he had near Buffalo, New York. While Sittler wasn't bragging, there was a whiff of self-importance at first meeting. Whether he intended to or not, he conveyed a sense that he was special, that his time in the NHL, particularly his years as captain of the Leafs, put him on a shelf above the rest of the guys.

Over coffee, for instance, Sittler happened to mention that the Leafs had just signed him to a new deal as a team ambassador, a role that included making public appearances on behalf of the team, talking to draft picks and offering advice on an as-needed basis. The Leafs, Sittler suggested, would have been crazy not to have given him a new deal.

"In terms of what I mean to the team," he said, "if they can pay Mats Sundin nine million dollars and Tie Domi two million, what they pay me is nothing when you consider what I mean to the city."

The thing is, of course, he was right. Sittler was like a god in Toronto. Even though he'd never brought a Stanley Cup to the city, he was revered for leading a team that was tough, colourful and not without talent. Unfortunately, throughout the 1970s, the team's biggest enemy was its owner—Harold Ballard, a miserly, miserable old coot who had no appetite for spending money on the kind of talented player that a team needed to win the Cup. So Sittler and Lanny McDonald and Tiger Williams and Borje Salming soldiered on, doing the best they could against ridiculous odds and a Montreal Canadiens dynasty that made most of the 1970s a race for second place in the NHL.

"Even though we didn't win all the time, fans enjoyed watching us," Sittler would say later, when we had a chance to talk about his time as a Leaf. "For lack of a better word, we were a blue-collar-type team that gave an honest effort most nights. Fans felt we had a chance.

"Of course, at the time Montreal had more depth than anyone, and then the Islanders came along after them and they were strong. But I think a lot of people feel that had they kept the nucleus of our team together and added a little more talent, we could have done something. But then Ballard brought Punch Imlach back, and he totally dismantled the team. The team went through this long period of turmoil and, I guess, insanity, that was so bad there were players who didn't even want to be drafted by the Leafs."

The Leafs sank to an all-time low in the early 1980s, the period Gary Nylund had described earlier. And Sittler believes that is one of the reasons the Leafs teams that he once led would be remembered so fondly—because fans were measuring their grit and heart and work ethic against the pathetic performances the team was giving them at the time.

By 1981, Sittler's relationship with Ballard had reached its lowest point. The owner was publicly questioning Sittler's leadership abilities, his heart, his character. Ballard had promised Sittler a new contract and then reneged, telling the Leafs captain that he would trade him to whichever team he wanted to go to. That was just the kind of nice guy Harold Ballard was.

"When he said that," Sittler remembered, "it was like taking something and piercing it through my heart. I said to Wendy, 'This is no fun. Let's go play where it's more fun. I can't stand this anymore.'"

And so it was that one of the most popular athletes in Leafs history, certainly one of the team's most popular captains, was traded to the Philadelphia Flyers for Rich Costello and a second-round draft choice. Three seasons later, Sittler's fifteen-year NHL career was over.

Sittler and his wife, Wendy, settled in East Amhurst, New York, after his career ended. He was anxious to make up for lost time with his three children, Ryan, Meaghan and Ashley. Given his high-profile career, Sittler became a natural pitchman for a number of companies. He had also made enough money that he could use a portion of his earnings to invest in various business opportunities and land-development proposals.

Although he had ended his career in the uniform of the Detroit Red Wings, Sittler knew there was only one team he would be identified with. And so, when Harold Ballard died and Steve Stavros bought the Maple Leafs and made Cliff Fletcher its general manager, Sittler saw this as a good sign. There had been no alumni association under Ballard, but under Stavros and Fletcher, establishing contact with every player who had ever worn a Leafs uniform became a priority. And Fletcher couldn't think of anyone better to represent the team's past than Sittler.

Sittler became a paid ambassador for the team and was once again seen on downtown Toronto streets, in restaurants and at games.

"It was great to be back in the organization," said Sittler. "After everything that happened with Ballard, and the way he treated me in the end, people in Toronto didn't forget. They knew how things ended and why they ended that way, and they never forgot the kind of team we were and the character we had.

"When I returned, I was treated so wonderfully by everyone I met. The young people who watched us play were in their late forties and early fifties now, with kids of their own. So, when they meet you now and they're with their kids, it's like: 'This is Darryl Sittler. He was one of the best Leafs ever' or 'He was one of my favourite players growing up.' That sort of thing. And you get it everywhere you go in Toronto."

But many kids already knew who Sittler was, thanks to the wild success of *My Leafs Sweater*, a children's book about the Leafs' captain's ten-point game.

"It's amazing how well that book has sold," Sittler said.

While making the NHL had always been Darryl Sittler's dream, becoming Toronto's captain would change his life. It many ways it defined him as a person, became an identity as recognizable as the Maple Leaf itself. Rejoining the organization allowed Sittler to come full circle with his team. It also allowed him to ultimately end the association on his terms, not someone else's.

Back in the Leafs fold, Sittler seemed to have it all: a gorgeous wife, three great children and enough money that he never had to worry about paying bills or maintaining a certain lifestyle. But a few years ago, Wendy Sittler was diagnosed with colon cancer, and suddenly Darryl Sittler felt like someone had cross-checked him headfirst into the boards.

"When you first get that kind of news, you're stunned," Sittler said. "Then you find out what you can about the disease, and you try and be hopeful that it can be beat. But honestly, it's like an anvil sitting over your head. You're just waiting for it to fall one day."

And on October 6, 2001, it fell.

Wendy Sittler's fight with cancer became a very public one in the end. She knew what she was up against. She also knew that the fame that surrounded her husband's name gave her an opportunity to raise awareness of this particular type of cancer that others could not. They held news conferences together. She had to talk.

"I had always been the front person before," said Sittler, remembering most of the public appearances he and his wife made over the years. "This time around, she was going to have to talk. And as nervous as it made her, she told me that if it helped save one person, than it was discomfort she could live with."

Darryl and Wendy Sittler were together for thirty years. There were times, he admitted, when their marriage wasn't as smooth as it might have appeared on the outside. But Darryl Sittler had never loved anyone so much in his life.

Wendy's funeral was held in East Amherst, at the church they attended most Sundays. By most accounts, it was as moving and wonderful a funeral service as there can be. Ardell McDonald, Lanny's wife, spoke. Darryl spoke. And everyone was shown a video, made by the Sittler children, that was intended as a lasting tribute to their mother. People sobbed. People laughed. That was the kind of service it was. And when it was over, Darryl Sittler went to his home and wondered how he would survive.

"Until it happens," Sittler told me as we talked about that day and the days that followed Wendy's death, "you don't know how you'll make it through. Nobody ever knows. But you just do it. It's like you get out of bed and put your clothes on, and you do whatever you have to do. And for the first few months I was just out of it, kind of in a fog wherever I was.

"But I'll tell you, when you have a nucleus of good friends, that really helps. Without their comfort and friendship, it would have been a hundred times harder. And I couldn't have done it without my faith. I do believe there is a God and he has a plan for us. I pray, and that helped me get through this too. But everybody grieves differently."

And Sittler has learned to grieve in his own way. As much as he misses his wife, Sittler prefers instead to think about the thirty years he had with her. And how thankful he should be for that. He also knows his wife wouldn't want him to mope around, feeling sorry for himself. That was one thing she made clear before she died.

"We had bought a place in Florida that we were really excited about," Sittler said. "It was a beautiful spot, big and right on the water. We picked everything out so that when it was finished we'd be ready to start putting the stuff in. We picked out the colours, the tiles, everything. Now that it's finished, I'm having to put all that stuff in that we had picked out together. So obviously I have huge mixed feelings about it. But I also know Wendy, and I know what she would be saying: 'Hey Darryl, enjoy it!'"

Florida seemed far away now. It was ten below outside in Red Deer and wouldn't be much warmer by the time we reached Calgary. But Sittler would be seeing his buddy Lanny, and anytime they got together it was good. It brought back the kinds of memories that sometimes eased the pain for Sittler but sometimes produced a tear or two as well.

"Lanny and I had some great times together," Sittler said as he got ready to see his friend. "We had some really good times."

CHAPTER 12

GILBERT PERREAULT SINGS ALOUETTE

I WASN'T SUITING UP for the game in Calgary. There were too many players. Lanny McDonald would be in the lineup for the Oldtimers, and they also had to give some shifts to a guy who paid three hundred dollars on eBay for the opportunity to play with the legends of hockey. There was also a reporter from Saskatoon along for a couple of games to write about the experience for his local paper, just as I had done myself a year earlier. With that many players, it made more sense for me to observe the game from the seats and to soak up a bit of the surroundings while I did.

I decided not to take the team bus from our hotel over to the Saddledome but instead to walk to the arena closer to game time. It was a warm March night, and as I turned the corner to head down the street that led to the Saddledome I couldn't believe my eyes. There were people—thousands of them. Streaming towards the doors of the arena like they did any night the hometown Flames were playing. Police were patrolling traffic. Cars were honking. People were waving. Young girls and young boys walked hand in hand. Mothers pushed strollers. Men wore old jerseys with names like Perreault and Sittler and McDonald on the back.

This was big.

By game time it seemed like the Saddledome was nearly full. And by seven o'clock people were on their feet whenever one of their favourite players was introduced. While McDonald was playing for the Oldtimers, the Calgary squad was a mix of RCMP officers and Flame alumni. Jamie Macoun was in uniform for them, as was Joel Otto and Dana Murzyn and Jim Peplinski. No game started, however, before Ron Hoggarth had a chance to introduce Bobby Hull to the crowd and they'd had a chance to go through their well-worn routine.

"Bobby Hull had a shot that was so hard he could shoot a puck through a car wash and it wouldn't even get wet," Hoggarth told the crowd.

"His brother Dennis had a harder shot than Bobby," Hoggarth continued before pausing. "He just couldn't hit the carwash."

And, of course, no conversation with Hull was complete without some mention of Brett. Being back in Calgary gave Hull the chance to remind everyone in the arena how the Flames blew it by allowing his child prodigy to be traded to the St. Louis Blues.

"Brett would go out and score two goals and then he'd be a healthy scratch the next night," Hull said, after commandeering Hoggarth's microphone. "I can't remember the name of the coach at the time, but can you imagine that? They used to say the reason they did it was so Brett would get mad and play better the next night."

Lanny McDonald looked great and could still skate. His moustache was as bushy as ever. His red hair was still long at the back but a little thinner at the front. Hoggarth brought Sittler and McDonald together for an interview, to the delight of the crowd, and Sittler's ten-point performance inevitably came up. McDonald had been on the ice for most of those points and had set up four of the six goals.

"It's a record that wasn't broken by Gretzky," McDonald told the crowd, "wasn't broken by Lemieux, and I don't think it will be broken ever unless Jarome Iginla gets hot one night."

The game was a special treat for the Oldtimers. Playing in front of so many people brought back great memories. Even getting to use an NHL-sized dressing room was a pleasure you could tell the players appreciated. "All this room!" Guy Lapointe exclaimed between periods. "This is more like it."

Given the number of former NHL players on the opposing team, the Oldtimers were expecting a battle. If any game was going to be tight, it was this one. And it was. The Oldtimers scored first, midway through the first period, but Calgary countered right back. The Oldtimers got up again, but the Flames alumni managed to deadlock the score 2–2 heading into the second period. The game remained close until midway through the second period, when the Oldtimers got two goals in just over a minute. A few minutes later they got another and that seemed to break the will of the gang from Calgary. The game became another Oldtimers romp.

In the dressing room afterwards, Saddledome staff brought down trays of sandwiches and vegetables. They also delivered heated containers of chicken wings that the guys dove into before they even had their equipment off.

It wouldn't be a dressing room, of course, unless someone was being victimized by a prank of sorts. And on this night it was a poor, unsuspecting Saddledome worker who was bringing down the food and whose job it was to inform the players of an even more elaborate buffet upstairs. It would be in the Air Canada Club lounge, where the post-game reception and autograph signing was scheduled to take place.

As the young man spoke, Richard Sevigny, the Quebec goaltender who was fluently bilingual, acted like he didn't quite understand what the man was saying.

"You have to tell him very slowly," one of the players told the

Saddledome worker. "He doesn't understand the language very well, so you need to tell him very slowly."

By now most of the guys were aware of the PIP—prank in progress—and turned their attention to the young man in the white server's uniform who was walking towards Sevigny to inform him where he needed to go after he got changed.

"Upstairs," the young man began and then stopped.

"THERE . . . IS . . . FOOD . . . FOR . . . YOU."

Sevigny shook his head like he didn't get it. The worker looked around for some guidance, and someone suggested he try again, even slower.

"FOOD," he began, miming someone eating.

"FOOD . . . UPSTAIRS," he continued, pointing heavenward.

The rest of the guys were now turning to one another, barely able to hold back their laughter while at the same time feeling sorry for the young kid. It was time to put him out of his misery.

"Oh," Sevigny finally said. "You're telling me there is food upstairs in the Air Canada lounge."

The poor kid's eyes grew wide, and everyone around him started laughing wildly. He slinked off with a couple of pats on the back from the guys.

In the Air Canada Club, members of the Flames alumni, guys like Murzyn and Otto and Peplinski, got caught up with players on the Oldtimers team whom they had played with or against at some time during their careers. McDonald and Sittler, meanwhile, sat at an autograph table talking to one another while constantly being interrupted by fans who wanted to take their picture. The crush of people in the lounge made it hot. Some of the players undid their shirt buttons and wiped any cold drink they could find across their forehead in an effort to cool down.

By midnight, there were still a hundred or so local fans who looked like they were going to stay as long as there were former NHL players in the room. But the guys looked tired, and pretty soon Jimmy Mann was rounding his people up to head to the bus and back to the hotel. A few of the players continued the party at a bar near the hotel, but most of us were happy to hit the sack.

"Seven A.M. in the lobby," Mann told the players on the bus.

The next day, the players wore predictably weary expressions. The bus ride to the Calgary airport, where we were to catch our mid-morning flight to Winnipeg, was exceptionally quiet—by Oldtimers standards. Once they got to the terminal and checked their hockey bags and other luggage, the guys hived off into groups of two or three to look for coffee and anything that resembled food. They killed time talking about their lives now, about old teammates and coaches. Telling all-time favourite stories.

Gilbert Perreault was telling some of the players that he now lived in Victoriaville, Quebec, and didn't work except for some appearances he did throughout the year on behalf of the Buffalo Sabres. He was talking about his former Sabres teammate Jim Schoenfeld when Reggie Leach joined the conversation to tell a story about the time he and Schoenfeld, both at the end of their careers, had played together in Detroit.

"One night he and Nick Pilano, the Wings' coach, were really going at it on the bench," Leach began. "They were just screaming at one another. Schoenfeld was saying, 'You're the worst coach I've ever had.' And Pilano was saying Schoenfeld was the worst player. Finally, Schoenfeld leaves the bench midway through the period—I can't remember which one—but he leaves the bench and goes to the dressing room.

"Apparently he threw his stick against the floor, and it popped right back up and hit the ceiling, setting off the fire sprinkler system. Well, pretty soon there is water everywhere. Schoenfeld goes out to alert the Joe Louis arena workers, but they can't find the valve to shut the sprinkler system off. By the time the period ends and we all file into the dressing room, there's five or six inches of water in the room. It was just a mess, but Schoeny got a good laugh out of it."

And, as always, one story led to another.

"Pilano was a real beauty," Leach continued. "Another time we were heading to Philly and it was the first time I played there since I left. It was near the end of the season and we were already out of it, so I decided to head out for a few. I get back to the hotel and it's two or three minutes past curfew and Pilano is waiting in the hotel lobby. So he says, that will cost you two hundred dollars, Reggie. I said: 'Fine, here's your two hundred bucks,' and I fished some bills out of my wallet, threw them at him and headed back out. I thought I'm already fined, might as well.

"So, I end up getting back at two or two-thirty in the morning, and Pilano is still waiting for me. So I'm really pissed off. As I say, there was only a few games left in the season and he's treating us like this. Anyway, he comes up to me and starts yelling at me so I call him an idiot. He says, 'What did you call me?' So I repeated it. Then he grabs me, so I popped him one right in the nose."

Needless to say, Leach didn't have his contract renewed the following season.

Bobby Hull, meantime, was looking particularly haggard.

"What time did you finally shut 'er down last night?" I asked him.

"Oh, about 5 A.M.," he replied.

Hull, as it turned out, hooked up with some friends that he knew from the cattle business. They hung around the Saddledome until they got kicked out and then found a downtown bar that was good enough to keep the booze flowing long after closing time. Such were the perks of being the Golden Jet. Or maybe of being the father of the Golden Brett.

Although most of the guys were tired, everyone still seemed to be in a good mood. Especially Perreault. The seats on the plane were assigned randomly and he and I lucked out, getting aisle seats right at the front of the plane. Perreault, I had been told, was a singer, but so far on the trip he had not entertained us with his dulcet tones. On the plane he broke out, first with several verses of the French-Canadian classic, "Alouette."

He didn't need a microphone. You could hear every "plu-merai" and "et la tête" in row 56. Perreault was every man in the shower, singing at the top of his lungs while he soaped up. After he was finished with "Alouette" he sang a Neil Diamond song, and after Neil Diamond it was something by Lionel Ritchie.

And all this happened before the flight had even taken off.

Finally, his choice of music struck the wrong chord with the flight attendant.

"Sex bombs, sex bombs!" Perreault screamed in his best Tom Jones impersonation.

Before he could go any further, the flight attendant gently informed Perreault that it probably wasn't the best song to be singing out loud on a plane. Not these days at least.

As I listened to Perreault, I realized how little we actually knew about our sports heroes. I mean, who would have known about this voice? A voice that could shatter windows at thirty thousand feet. For some reason I had always thought of Perreault as a shy, certainly reserved, superstar who never seemed interested in grabbing as much of the limelight as he could. But what a player. His years with René Robert and Rick Martin as the French Connection Line produced some of the most exciting hockey ever played.

"I was there to make the plays," Perreault would explain. "Rick was there to score the goals, and René could do a little of both."

You see so few players like Perreault anymore. He was one of the last forwards in the game who could pick up the puck behind his net and skate through an entire team before leaving it in the opposition's net for some poor goalie to fish out. It's not that today's players aren't as skilled, Perreault will quickly admit, it's just that there is so much more hooking and grabbing and clogging up of the neutral zone that it's impossible to play the game like it once was played.

It took the Sabres only five years to get to the Stanley Cup finals from the time they joined the NHL in 1970 and made

Perreault the number one pick overall. That year they faced off against the Philadelphia Flyers, getting up two games to none. But then Bernie Parent became unbeatable and Philly won the next four straight, and that was as close as Perreault would ever get to the Cup.

"I always show Perreault my Stanley Cup ring from that year and rub it in," Moose Dupont, who patrolled the Flyers blueline that season, would tell me later in the trip.

"I say, 'Gilbert, this is your ring.'"

Perreault just shakes his head.

Moose Dupont was a funny guy too. When you met him it was hard to imagine this was the same guy in the middle of all those bench-clearing brawls that the Philadelphia Flyers tended to incite in the 1970s. He looked more like a high school math teacher, with his short brown hair and wireframe glasses, but when he played Dupont was a tough as they came. And although he wasn't the best fighter of his day, there wasn't a player he ever backed down from.

Moose sat down beside me for some of the flight to Winnipeg and talked about Fred Shero, the legendary Flyers coach, and Bernie Parent and Kate Smith, who used to sing "God Bless America" before the games at the Spectrum in Philly and work the crowd into a state of absolute madness.

"Those crowds in Philly were wild then," Moose told me above the din of the plane's engines. "They used to stand and cheer for the warm-up. The entire warm-up they were going crazy. The other teams just hated playing at the Spectrum because it was always so loud, and it could get real crazy there."

Moose was right. No one liked playing in Philly. And the truth was, no one particularly liked playing Philly either. The Flyers were big and mean and dirty and did anything to win. Intimidation was an essential element of their game. Moose laughed at the story I'd heard about Pierre Larouche, the talented but soft forward from Quebec who played for the Pittsburgh Penguins in the mid-1970s, when the Flyers were at their scariest.

Larouche, just out of junior, found himself in the faceoff circle against Bobby Clarke.

"Touch that puck and we'll smash your head in," Clarke was alleged to have told Larouche before the puck was dropped.

"No problem, Bobby," Larouche replied. "It's all yours."

Moose snickered. "And Pierre Larouche wouldn't have been the only one to say that."

Moose said the Broad Street Bullies, as the team became known for their style of play and the street location of their arena in Philadelphia, were like a family. The players stood behind each other, and when it was time to go to war, you pitched in whenever you could, however you could.

"I remember one time we were playing Boston, I think," Moose recalled. "Yes, Boston. And a brawl erupted and the benches cleared. Our defenceman Eddie Van Impe tried to jump over the boards to join the fray and slipped. He somehow got wedged in between the bench and the boards and couldn't get out. But he still had his stick in his hand, so anytime two guys who were fighting got close to him, Eddie was using his stick to spear one of the Bruins' guys.

"He was asking for help from the bench and we were like, 'Eddie, can't you see? We're a little tied up at the moment.' Eddie was a little dirtier than some of the guys. During brawls he would come over to see how you were making out and then would give the guy you were fighting a little jab in the ribs with his stick. And he'd say, 'Are you doing better now?' And we always were because the guy we were fighting could barely breathe."

THE FLIGHT TO The Peg was smooth. Gilbert Perreault continued to sing. Sheets of paper were passed around for the players to sign. The rest of the passengers on the flight were now aware of who they were flying with and wanted something to prove it when they landed.

After landing we hopped on a bus and headed directly for the Winnipeg Arena. It would be a special night for a couple of people on the team—Dale Hawerchuk and Bobby Hull—who had both played major roles in the city's hockey scene. The crowd always had a soft spot in its heart for a tough guy too, so Jimmy Mann, who had been the team's resident goon for the first half of the 1980s, was expected to get a boisterous response from the crowd when he skated onto the ice that evening.

But nothing like Hull and Hawerchuk.

Hull, of course, helped put Winnipeg on the hockey map by defecting to the Jets and the World Hockey Association in the 1970s. Hawerchuk arrived nearly ten years later, the first overall pick in the NHL draft, a highly skilled centre who had been heralded as the second coming of Wayne Gretzky as a junior.

Hull had been to Winnipeg several times before with the tour, so the feeling wasn't quite as odd for him. But this was Hawerchuk's first return to the city in a while, and he wasn't quite sure what to expect. All he knew was that the visit was sure to stir up some old memories.

As the bus turned the corner and the Winnipeg Arena came into sight, someone yelled out: "There it is, the house that Dale Hawerchuk built and Jimmy Mann destroyed." Everyone laughed, even Jimmy.

Inside, the old rink still looked pretty good. And if you closed your eyes for a minute, you could hear eighteen thousand screaming people, all wearing white. It could get loud in here, Bobby Hull said as we looked around together.

"There used to be a picture of the queen right up there," he said, pointing to a spot at the south end of the arena, right above the first section of seating. "We used to fire shots from centre ice and try and hit the picture. And if you ever looked at it closely, you could see puck marks all over her."

The arena was now home to the Manitoba Moose, the farm team of the Vancouver Canucks. All the talk in the city was about a new arena planned for downtown. It wasn't a sure lock, but people were hopeful it would go ahead and help revitalize the city's stagnant downtown core.

Dale Hawerchuk looked around the old arena, twenty years after first pulling a Jets jersey over his head, and could remember his first game here like it was yesterday.

"I can remember everything about walking through that runway for my first game," he said as he looked around at the empty seats. "There was a song by Kenny Loggins that had come out around then, called "This Is It." And I remember it going through my mind as I stood in the hallway waiting to go out on the ice. The day I had dreamed about my whole life had finally arrived. I was in the NHL. Now it was time to go out and do something about it."

Hawerchuk hadn't been so sure weeks before his NHL debut. Arriving for training camp, with all the baggage that a first overall pick carries to the big leagues, he was frightened to death. He remembered taking his first skate as a training camp rookie, suddenly afraid that he didn't have the speed or the strength to keep up with the other players.

"I remember going back to my hotel room after that first day of training camp feeling really down," Hawerchuk recalled. "I was thinking, here I was, a first overall pick, and I wasn't going to make it. But I kept working at it, and eventually I started to feel better and began to feel like I fit in. Within a couple of weeks I was humming along quite nicely."

One day, shortly after arriving at camp, Hawerchuk and teammate Scott Arniel decided to unwind in the hot tub back at the hotel. Both were young stars in junior who were excited about the team the Jets would have that year—a team they both felt could do some damage in the playoffs. However, there was someone else in the hot tub who didn't share their enthusiasm.

"This guy pipes up and starts talking about what a crappy team we were going to have," Hawerchuk recalled. "Arniel and I are sort of looking at ourselves, like, who is this guy to say we're going to be lousy. And then we go to this team orientation meeting the next day, and who should be sitting at the head table with the rest of the coaches and management but the guy in the hot tub. As it turned out it was Mike Smith, who would later become the GM of the team but was then a scout or something. Arniel and I looked at one another and thought, 'Oh, oh. If this is the kind of person they have working for this organization we're in trouble.' Never liked Mike Smith."

The first few years in Winnipeg were a blast for Hawerchuk. His first season as a pro he managed to live up to all the hype that surrounded his arrival in the league, scoring 45 goals and adding 58 assists for 103 points. It was good enough to earn him the Calder Trophy as the top rookie in the league. Life was good.

"There was a group of us those first few years—Scott Arniel, Jim Kyte, Brian Mullen and myself—that all hung out together," said Hawerchuk, smiling at the memory. "I bought this house and we all lived in it. We had a great time. I remember we used to go out to the parks and we'd take our skates and sticks and play outdoor hockey with the kids. Then the kids would figure out who we were, and all of a sudden there would be forty kids, and the parents would start showing up with cameras. We'd play until eleven o'clock and even midnight sometimes, and then the next day we'd have a practice or a game.

"We were all twenty and under, and so into hockey that that's all we knew. That's all we wanted to do, play hockey. It would be forty below, but we didn't care. We'd go out and play."

Hawerchuk went on to have several outstanding seasons with Winnipeg, highlighted by a 53-goal, 77-assist, 130-point campaign in 1984–85. But as wonderful as that season was, Hawerchuk lived in the era of Gretzky, and the same year The Great One had

208 points. The Jets, despite making continual strides in the years immediately after Hawerchuk's arrival, could never make an impact in the post-season. Getting to the Stanley Cup finals was a particular problem for teams in the West, who had to get by Gretzky's Oilers and the always-powerful Calgary Flames.

Eventually the guy in the hot tub, Mike Smith, took over as the Jets GM, and Hawerchuk knew his time as a Jet would soon be over.

"I thought I'd give him a chance," Hawerchuk said, a few hours before Winnipeg fans would be welcoming him back. "But I could tell things weren't going anywhere here, and it was time to move on. Smith asked me where I wanted to go. I said 'Toronto,' and he said, 'No way, I'm not trading you to the Leafs.' Finally, I said, 'Go find a deal,' and so in the summer of 1990 he did a deal with Buffalo for Phil Housley, and I became a Sabre."

Hawerchuk would have four strong seasons with Buffalo but never get to the Stanley Cup finals. The Sabres had the worst luck with injuries. The one season that the team had the best chance of actually going somewhere in the playoffs, its core group of stars—Pat LaFontaine, Alexander Mogilny and goalie Grant Fuhr—got hurt. At the time, the team decided to let Fuhr battle through an ankle injury rather than give its little-known and just-traded-for backup a chance to carry the goaltending load. In retrospect, Hawerchuk said, that might have been a mistake.

The backup was Dominik Hasek.

After Buffalo, Hawerchuk would make stops in St. Louis and Philadelphia before calling it a career. He would finish with 1,188 career games in the NHL, becoming the youngest player to reach the thousand-game milestone. His sixteen-year Hall of Fame resume would include 518 goals, 891 assists and 1,409 points. Ironically, his last year in the league would be the first year of the Jets' existence in their new home of Phoenix. And while the move came as a shock to many, it didn't to Hawerchuk.

"I could see it coming," he said, shaking his head. "Let me tell you something. People who live in Winnipeg, Calgary and Edmonton are a certain type of people. They're really honest, enjoyable people. What they demand is an honest day's work. They don't necessarily care if you win or lose, just that you give them an honest day's effort.

"After Mike Smith took over as GM he brought in fifteen European imports, and for Winnipeggers to come out and watch them cruise around and lose was just unacceptable. They could have watched twenty western Canadian boys go out and work their butts off and lose, and they would have supported that. But they weren't going to support the team Smith put on the ice. People forget that in the years before the team left, the crowds were really down in Winnipeg. And when that happens in a market like this, it's tough. The only reason they came back is the people realized they were going to steal their team, and they got scared and came out. But it was the product that got the ball rolling."

Later that night, Dale Hawerchuk skated out on the ice at Winnipeg Arena to the loudest ovation of the evening. Some stood. Some held signs. And somewhere in the crowd, a father was telling his son about the night he played hockey with the former Jets star—under twinkling stars and a bright, clear moon—and the thought of losing him and the team one day was unimaginable.

THE RIVERTON RIFLE

REGGIE LEACH FIRST drank when he was 12.

Lots of people drank in Riverton, the small community two hours north of Winnipeg where Leach grew up. And kids tended to do it too in the 1950s and 1960s.

Leach, a member of the Barens River Indian band, grew up in what he would later describe as a "typical" native family. His mother was a teenager when she had Reggie on April 23, 1950. The boy's father was also a teenager, one who had no means of supporting a family. So a decision was made to put the baby up for adoption—by Reggie's grandparents.

"There were thirteen of us when I was growing up," said the former Philadelphia Flyer.

The Oldtimers' plane from Winnipeg touched down early on a Sunday morning in the B.C. capital. A bus took us to our hotel, the Chateau Victoria, where the players dispersed in different directions. Some headed for their rooms to grab some sleep; others headed off in search of food. Leach and I decided to test the grub at the hotel, which had two restaurants—VISTA 18—which offered a stunning view of the city harbour from the eighteenth floor and Victoria Jane's, which was less dynamic and breathtaking and situated on the main floor. We opted for the understated darkness of Victoria Jane's, which had a table just for us near the back.

"I was adopted at six months, so I always knew my grandparents as Mom and Dad," Leach continued. "My brothers and sisters were really my uncles and aunts, I guess, but they were just brothers and sisters to me. I didn't know any different. I was the only one that was adopted. One of my twelve brothers and sisters was actually my father.

"That's what I call a typical native family. It happens quite often, where the parents can't look after a child, so it's adopted by the grandparents. I would say 90 to 95 per cent of the time they won't let the child be adopted by someone outside the band. Natives take care of their own. But it was tough growing up. We had no money. We grew up on welfare, and if you can believe it, our house only had two bedrooms and no plumbing. So you can imagine what that was like growing up. It was pretty crowded."

Reggie Leach didn't learn to skate until he was ten. The first pair of skates he ever wore were several sizes too big, so he stuffed socks in the toes to make them fit. Within a few years, though, young Reggie Leach was the talk of the town, and he was so good that he was even playing with the local senior men's team.

"I used to sneak into the rink at two o'clock in the morning," Leach said, as coffee arrived. "I would have the place all to myself. At thirteen I was playing games with the senior men's team. There was always drinking going on there, so I got into it. But I'd already started drinking at twelve. It wasn't a big deal then."

When Leach was fourteen, he went to Lashburn, Saskatchewan, to play Junior B hockey. By Christmas he was homesick and back in Riverton, happy to finish out the season playing for the senior men's team he'd played with before. That summer, a man named Siggi Johnson dropped by Leach's house to talk to the boy he'd coached for three seasons in minor hockey.

"We're going for a ride," Siggi said to Leach as they walked out of the house.

They headed to the local restaurant, where Siggi bought Reggie a Coke. Then he got down to business.

"Reggie," Siggi said. "What do you want to do with your life?"

"I want to be a hockey player," Reggie said.

Siggi paused for a second and then looked the young boy sitting across from him straight in the eyes.

"If you want to play hockey you've got to get out of this town, Reggie," said Siggi. "If you don't, you're going to end up just like the kids on the road out there. They could have been hockey players too, but they didn't leave. You have to."

After five minutes, Reggie Leach knew Siggi was right. He had to leave Riverton—for good.

Within a month, Leach had packed his bags and was on the bus to Flin Flon, Manitoba, where he had a tryout with the Bombers of the Manitoba junior league. At training camp, Leach would meet a local kid also trying out for the team—Bobby Clarke. It would be the start, as they say, of a beautiful relationship.

In their first season together, Leach and Clarke, both sixteen years old, would lead the Bombers to a Memorial Cup. Leach, moved up to the wing from defence, where he normally played, became a terror teamed with Clarke. In his first year Leach—who had been dubbed the Riverton Rifle for his amazing speed and blazing shot—scored 45 goals and 67 assists for 113 points. Clarke's output was even more stunning: he scored 71 goals and assisted on 112 others to gain a staggering 183 points.

The following season, Leach would set a league record for most goals, with 87. Two years after that he was the third overall pick in the 1970 NHL draft and was selected by the then-mighty Boston Bruins.

"Boston was not a good experience," Leach said, leaning back in his chair for a moment. "I didn't play, and that wasn't good. I knew I was better than some of the guys on the Bruins, but I couldn't get in the lineup that first season. They sent me down to Oklahoma for a bit, and then in the second season I didn't get any time when I did dress. So, all in all, it wasn't a good scene, and that's really when trouble started."

And Reggie Leach started drinking—hard.

Leach's fire for the game had been partially doused by the experience in Boston. He was bitter. Increasingly, he drank to soothe his wounded pride. On February 23, 1972, he was traded to the California Golden Seals with Rick Smith and Bob Stewart for Carol Vadnais and Don O'Donoghue. Although Leach was happy that he was going to a team he knew would play him, Oakland wasn't exactly a hockey hotbed.

Leach continued to drink while his production continued to fall far below expectations. In his first full season with the Seals he compiled a listless 35 points and in his second season a lethargic 46. But his luck was about to change.

On May 24, 1974, Leach was traded to the Philadelphia Flyers for Larry Wright, Al MacAdam and Philly's first-round draft choice in that year's draft—a pick that ended up being Ron Chipperfield. As soon as he received the news, Reggie Leach could think of only one person.

Bobby Clarke.

Although Leach suspected that Clarke had something to do with the trade, his former centre with the Flin Flon Bombers denied it. Regardless, their old chemistry was still there, and in their first NHL season together Leach began to return to form. In 80 games, Leach scored 45 goals and added 33 assists. Leach, Clarke and Bill Barber combined for 265 points that season to become one of the most dangerous lines in the NHL.

Leach would add ten more points that year during a playoff

march that went all the way to the Stanley Cup finals. And for the second year in a row, the Flyers bullied and scored their way to another championship title, this time over the Buffalo Sabres.

It was the first Stanley Cup showdown between two expansion teams. Bobby Clarke headed into the final as the Hart Trophy winner as the best player of the year, for the second straight season. And Bernie Parent was going into the matchup as the Vézina Trophy winner as the league's best goaltender.

This would be the series that Moose Dupont would rib Gilbert Perreault about. The series that Buffalo got up 2–0 on Philadelphia before promptly dropping the next four. Other than being the Flyers' second consecutive Stanley Cup win, the series would be remembered for the fog that rose from the ice at Buffalo's Memorial Auditorium and frequently interrupted play.

Playing a pivotal role on a Stanley Cup–calibre team helped Leach get over some of the bitterness he had been feeling before his trade from California. But by then, he had become too close with the bottle to let it go completely. He could still hit it pretty hard, and it wasn't uncommon for Leach to show up for practices drunk or with a hangover.

His second season with the Flyers would be Leach's best. In 1975–76, he scored 61 goals and 30 assists. Philadelphia, meantime, enjoyed another outstanding season, leading the Patrick Division with 118 points. In that year's playoffs, the Flyers met the Toronto Maple Leafs in the quarter-finals and won. It was in the next series against Boston that Reggie Leach made history, scoring five goals in one game. Even more amazing was how he did it.

Dead drunk.

It wasn't the first time Leach had shown up at the rink for a game after drinking all afternoon. But this was different. This was the playoffs.

"Freddy Shero wasn't going to let me play," Leach recalled.

"Clarke was saying, 'Let him play, let him play, he'll be fine. He knew that I played drunk before. I would always say to him, just get me the puck and I'll be fine.'"

In the end, Clarke prevailed. Leach played, scoring five times on six shots, and the Flyers won.

In fact, Reggie Leach played brilliantly throughout that post-season. In sixteen playoff games he scored nineteen goals, an NHL record he still shares today with Edmonton's Jari Kurri. Even though the Flyers didn't win the Stanley Cup that season, Leach was still awarded the Conn Smythe as the top performer in the playoffs. It was the first time anyone other than a goalie had won the award playing for a team that didn't win the Cup.

It would be Reggie Leach's last great season with the Flyers. After his 91-point campaign in 1975–76, Leach's production began to fall again. The following season he managed only 46 points, the one after that 52, then 54. He rebounded briefly later in the decade, when he had 76- and 70-point seasons respectively in 1979–80 and 1980–81. But by then his drinking problem was out of control.

The following season, Flyers coach Pat Quinn was fired and replaced by Bob "Cagey" McCammon. The year before, Leach had signed a one-year contract that stipulated that if he scored 30 goals or 50 points it would be extended for two more years. In 66 games, Leach had scored 26 goals and added 21 assists for 47 points. Before the sixty-seventh game, he was called into McCammon's office and told he was being released.

"They said they were going to try and trade me at first, but the trade deadline came and went and nothing happened," Leach said, as he mixed his salad up with a fork. "Anyway, McCammon called me in and said, 'Go home, we don't want you anymore.' That was it essentially."

The following year, Leach signed as a free agent with the Detroit Red Wings. He would score a measly 15 goals and 17 assists for 32 points, his most anemic output since his first year in the league when he got six points in twenty-three games for the Bruins. Leach's hockey career was over. He would spend the next season with the Montana Magic in the Central Hockey League. By then he was a curiosity more than anything.

The year in Montana was nothing but a party. Reggie Leach was drinking harder than ever. A year later he was divorced and handed virtually everything he owned over to his ex-wife. Over the years he had tried to stop drinking, but always for someone else—his wife, his team, his kids—never for himself. Which is why he was never successful in beating back the demons that followed him wherever he went.

One day, Reggie Leach woke up scared. He shook uncontrollably. He was cold and sick. This had never happened before, even after his worst benders. The next thing he knew, he was in a hospital, talking to a doctor.

"Reggie," the doctor said, "you have done some serious damage to your liver. Now you have a choice."

Leach sat silent.

"And your choice is you can live or you can die."

"What do you mean?" Leach asked him.

"What I mean is, your liver can't take much more abuse, and when it stops working that's it. It's over."

The doctor asked Leach if he wanted help trying to stop. This time Reggie Leach answered for himself, not anyone else.

"Yes, I do," he said.

Leach was in a rehab clinic the next day. He hasn't had a drink since.

The first two years of sobriety were the worst. Or at least the hardest. When he returned to the Philadelphia area to begin the next phase of his life, to find a job and settle down, he would often find himself in the company of old teammates, at charity golf tournaments, for instance. After the round, everyone would inevitably end up in the bar, where drinks were inevitably foisted on Leach. Saying "no" was never easy, especially when certain friends kept insisting that one drink wouldn't be a problem. But other former teammates, guys like Dave "The Hammer" Schultz, understood exactly what Leach was going through and would often intervene when others kept trying to put a drink in Leach's hands. "Hey," Schultz would say. "He said he doesn't want a drink. Leave him alone."

Today, Leach has a small landscaping company that he runs in Philadelphia. He is happily remarried. He has mended relations with his kids, who resented their father for years. And he spends several days a year on reserves in Canada telling his story and showing young native kids all the potholes you can step into on the road of life.

"I now have what I call the three lives of Reggie Leach," said Leach, as more coffee arrived.

"I have my hockey life, which is the alumni games that I play in and charity appearances and tours like this. I have my native life, which is when I go out to the reserves and talk about drugs and alcohol and stuff. And I have today's life, which is my wife and my family and my landscaping business.

"The biggest thing right now is the middle one. I feel so strongly about trying to keep kids from making the same mistake I did. And I tell them about my mistakes. I tell them what alcohol can do to you. How alcohol can hurt you in the long run. How it hurt me. But I also tell them how I stopped. How I beat alcohol, and how it changed my life in the process. My big thing is choices. We all have choices to make. Everyone has dreams and goals, and everyone has to make choices in pursuit of them."

Leach took a final swig of his coffee, set down his cup and smiled.

"You know what I say now? There's never a bad day in my life . . . Some days are just better than others."

Later that evening, the Oldtimers took to the ice against their latest victims, a team comprised of local police and firefighters. This was the fourth game since the team had first come together in Red Deer, and the players were getting much more comfortable with one another. It wasn't like the Oldtimers team that had explored the far north together, or for that matter, even like the group that was joined together in the B.C. Interior, but you could tell that all it took was three or four days in planes and buses and dressing rooms to bring a group of hockey players together.

"Hey, Moose, no passes to the other team tonight," barked Gilbert Perreault.

"*Tabernac,*" came the response. "Don't you worry about me. They never score on us when I'm on the ice."

"That's because you ask to come off so quickly," someone else said.

"*Tabernac.*"

The game in Victoria was the most lopsided affair of the entire tour. The Oldtimers could have scored forty goals on the overmatched opposition and did everything they could to hold the total to fifteen. It was the kind of game, though, that Reggie Leach shone in. His once-blazing speed was still evident. It was hard not to smile when he raced down the ice, his trademark mullet still blowing in the wind behind him. He would score four goals.

And the best part was, he did it sober.

CHAPTER 14

THE LAST SHIFT

This was it.

It was a beautiful west coast March morning as our bus pulled into the ferry terminal a half hour outside Victoria. We were headed to Vancouver, my final stop on the tour. We had about a thirty-minute wait at the terminal before boarding the ferry and the ninety-minute ride to the B.C. mainland, so we all got off the bus and stretched our legs and looked around at the water and the birds that flew overhead. More than a few of us took off our jackets and lifted our faces up towards a bright, warm sun.

Although the guys had three more stops after Vancouver, I was getting off. I had mixed feelings about it. The tour could be a grind, and late nights and early mornings could wear on you after a while, but there was something intoxicating about it, too. Being on the bus, listening to conversations, sharing beers and jokes and songs was fun. In some ways the tour was like a rolling party, one you didn't want to leave.

I realized as I stood there outside the bus how many wonderful people I'd met since I first laced up my skates with the Oldtimers back in November. Some of the guys were big-name stars in their day, but many were not. That's not to say they weren't just as lucky as the Hockey Hall of Famers, because Marc Bureau and Wayne Babych and Doug Bodger could say the same thing as Bobby Hull and Marcel Dionne and Darryl Sittler—they played in the NHL, one of the most exclusive clubs in the world.

Travelling with the Oldtimers certainly gave me a taste of this exclusive club. Although an uncommon competitive zeal is what drives anyone who makes it as far as the big leagues, it's the brotherhood, the chatter in the dressing room, the laughs and beer after the game that make the experience truly wonderful. In only a few months, I came to understand why it is so hard for hockey players to hang up their skates: for most players, nothing they do after they retire will come close to what they did while they played.

Outside the bus, Peter Stastny was talking to his brother, Anton. I had wanted to talk to Peter for days and hadn't really had the chance. The two brothers had been inseparable since Red Deer, sitting with one another on the bus and the airplane and in restaurants. Peter lived in St. Louis now, and Anton in Switzerland, so they hadn't seen one another in a while and there was some catching up to do. Unlike some of the other players who had retired from the game years ago, both of the Stastnys were remarkably fit. Peter became had become a target of abuse on the trip for his penchant for stepping on the bus at precisely the moment it was scheduled to leave. If we were due, for instance, to pull away from some city at 9:15 A.M., Stastny would emerge from the front of the hotel at 9:14.55, and everyone would razz him as he stepped aboard.

"Hey, Peter, you're early!" someone would yell. "You still have three seconds."

Neither of the Stastnys really looked like hockey players. There wasn't a rough edge to either of them. They both looked like they could have been doctors or people who made their livelihoods in the world of high finance. There was something almost aristocratic about them, and the fact that they were both so articulate contributed to that feeling.

Finding Peter standing alone for a minute, I decided to go up and chat. I had wanted to hear the story first-hand of his and Anton's 1980 escape from Czechoslovakia that had brought them to Canada and the NHL. The Stastnys had another brother, Marian, who would also join them in the NHL but not until eight months after their escape.

As we stood outside, occasionally glancing up at the sun to fight off the morning chill, Peter told me that he first became aware of the shortcomings of the communist regime in Czechoslovakia in his late teens and early twenties. By then, he and his brothers were playing for Slovakia in the Czech league, and their team was becoming a powerhouse thanks in large part to the Stastnys. Then the Stastnys led their team to a national championship—the first time a team from Slovakia had ever done so, and the last time for years to come.

Czech authorities didn't like the idea of the Slovaks winning the national championship, so they decided to take measures to ensure that it didn't happen again. The following year, players who had been part of the big Slovak win were suddenly no longer with the team.

"They took four or five guys off our team because the Czechs didn't want to lose the national championship again," said Stastny. "Suddenly, guys on our team weren't good enough anymore. There were a lot of dirty, dirty things going on. We didn't like it. I knew what it took to win. But their attitude was, as long as the Slovaks have the Stastnys they'll be fine. But doing fine wasn't good enough. We wanted to win.

"But the Czech authorities discovered a gold mine in trading and selling players. There was a lot, a lot, of money involved in every transaction. It was contrary to what I believed. I started to stand up against what I saw going on. I wasn't afraid. After the 1980 Olympics I decided I couldn't stand it anymore. I had to defect."

You live only once, Stastny thought. And at this point in his early twenties, newly married with a child on the way, he knew he didn't want his children raised in that environment. The ideals promoted by Czechoslovakia's communist government were contrary to the values he was raised to believe in, values he intended to pass along to his own children.

"I was worried that my children would grow up hypocrites," Stastny remembered as he looked out at the water. "I could see myself teaching them one thing at home, and as soon as they got out of the home, or at school or everywhere else, they'd be taught something else. That was a terrible picture for me, and I knew that was going to be a terrible thing for me. I knew that as soon as I was done hockey, the advantages that I had would be gone and I would no longer be good enough."

In 1976, the Stastnys played for Czechoslovakia in the Canada Cup. All three brothers caught the attention of NHL scouts. In 1979, the Quebec Nordiques, perhaps playing a hunch, decided to draft Anton, even though there was no guarantee that he would ever leave his homeland. It turned out to be a lucrative hunch, even though Peter and his brothers worried about what might happen if they defected.

"I knew it would be difficult," Stastny recalled. "I knew it would cause a lot of harm and pain and grief and wouldn't be easy. The communists were monsters. Maybe they couldn't get you, but they could get people who knew you. Your family. So very often you would think about defecting and then decide no.

"The other thing was, we were treated like royalty. We had everything we wanted, and the status in our society was so high we had to ask ourselves what else could we gain by being over here. But eventually your competitive juices get flowing, and you want to try the NHL. You want to measure yourself against the best players in the world."

When the Czech authorities arranged for seven players from another strong Slovak team to be traded, that was it for Peter Stastny. He knew he would have to go. So did Anton. It was more difficult for Marian, who had a wife and children; it wouldn't be so easy for him just to pick up and leave. Anytime he left the country to play, the authorities never allowed his children to travel with him, so there was no way to ensure a safe passage for them. Peter and Anton knew that if they were going to leave, they would have to leave their older sibling behind.

And it was now or never.

In the summer of 1980, the Slovaks travelled to Innsbruck, Austria, to play in a tournament. Peter phoned the Quebec Nordiques and told them that he and Anton were ready to defect. It was around noon in Austria when Stastny placed the call to Nordiques officials, late evening back in Quebec. He thought it might take the team a couple of days to get something organized, but by early the next morning the Nordiques returned his call.

"I couldn't believe it," Stastny said. "It was still dark outside. They had all the information and the plans and how it would all work. I asked when they would be arriving, and they said: 'No, we're already here. We're in the hotel across the street.' I couldn't believe it. It was so fast. I nearly dropped the phone."

As the final pieces of the escape plan fell into place, the Stastnys continued to play for their team. Meantime, they worked with the Nordiques officials to iron out contracts. They eventually worked out a deal for everyone—including Marian, when and if he arrived in Canada. The Stastnys arrived back at their hotel around 10:30 P.M., following their team's last game of the tournament. The team bus was supposed to leave shortly after midnight.

The plan was for the brothers to leave the hotel through a back door, where a car would be waiting to take them away. But when it came time to leave, Anton was nowhere to be found.

"I couldn't believe it," said Stastny, remembering that night more than twenty years earlier. "I couldn't find Anton anywhere. We looked and looked around the hotel. Nowhere. I'll tell you, it was one of the most horrifying times in my life. I was worried that the secret service had gotten to him. There were always strange and suspicious looking people hanging around the team. You never really knew who worked for the communists, who was their extra eye. I was worried that they had snatched him."

Now it was close to 1:30 in the morning, long after they were supposed to leave the hotel. Peter Stastny and the Nordiques could wait no longer. It was either go now or stay behind and try it another time. Peter mulled it over for a while and decided he would go, confident that his brother would reappear at some point or make contact with someone to let them know where he was.

"We began driving through downtown Innsbruck," Stastny said. "And we were on this road heading out of town, and in the distance I saw the silhouette of this person walking along the side of the road. At first I thought it was just my imagination, that I was dreaming. I thought it was a mirage or something. But as we got closer I realized I wasn't dreaming." It was Anton.

Somehow there had been a mixup in communications. Anton had thought that he was supposed to meet the team officials somewhere else. It didn't matter now. The two brothers rode in the back of the car, scared, elated, worried, anxious and more nervous than they'd ever been for a hockey game. They drove over the mountains to Vienna, where they were taken to a hotel. Undercover agents scurried all over the place, sweeping the place for electronic listening devices.

"It was like out of a James Bond movie," said Stastny. "I'd never seen anything like it in my life. My wife was with me, and we say that is why she delivered the baby three weeks early—because of the whole experience with the escape."

It wouldn't take long for Peter and Anton to make an impact in the NHL. In his first season, Anton would score 39 goals and add 46 assists for 85 points. Peter, meanwhile, would equal his brother's goal production but have 70 assists for a rookie-best 109 points. And at twenty-five years of age, he was named the NHL's rookie of the year.

Back in Bratislava, Czech authorities, angered by the high-profile defections of two of their country's top athletes, decided to take their frustration out on the Stastny brother who had remained. It wasn't long before the communists stripped Marian of virtually every right he had in the country. Police followed him and interrogated everyone he came in contact with. Gradually, he lost all his friends. They were not up for the psychological warfare that the communists had launched against Marian and those around him.

Behind the scenes, Nordiques officials continued to work on a plan to get Marian and his wife and children out. That summer, Peter and Anton were in Las Vegas for a meeting of the NHL Players' Association when they were passed news that Marian was in Vienna. He was getting out. "You can't imagine how we felt," Peter said with a broad smile. "We knew they were working on something, but you never know if it's going to work out. When we found out he was safe, it was just an unbelievable feeling."

And Peter and Anton could finally get rid of the guilt they both had carried with them since fleeing to Vienna themselves nine months earlier.

"I can tell you, I felt very responsible for what was happening to Marian back home," Peter said, suddenly becoming quite serious. "Some people may have viewed what we did as selfish. I didn't want to leave, but it was a dilemma I had to wrestle with for a long time before making the decision." The Stastnys' parents stayed behind. It was rough at first; they were interrogated at every turn, just as anyone they talked to was.

Stastny's father lost a promotion he was due. Eventually, however, things got better and the parents were allowed to travel back and forth between Czechoslovakia and Canada, where they came to watch their sons play in the NHL and enjoy time with their grandchildren.

Although all three Stastnys made an impact in Quebec, Peter emerged as a legitimate NHL superstar. He would collect one hundred or more points seven times in his fifteen-year career, and he was in the top ten in scoring six times—finishing second behind Wayne Gretzky in 1982–83. He played in six All-Star games.

In 1990, Peter was traded to the New Jersey Devils. By then, his best days were behind him. After the breakup of the Soviet Union, he returned to Slovakia and played for the independent country's national team at the 1994 Lillehammer Olympics, where he was his team's captain and his country's flag-bearer. He returned to the NHL as a free agent in 1993–94, signing with the St. Louis Blues. He ended up retiring for good the following year. His great career was highlighted in 1998, when he was elected to the Hockey Hall of Fame.

But the highlight of his life had happened years earlier, after the Velvet Revolution had ended communist rule in Czechoslovakia: he was able to return to his homeland, with his children, without fear of reprisal. "I had four children by then," Stastny said. "The youngest was five and the oldest was ten. It was a great feeling to be able to show them where I was from. For them to see things that were just pictures in a book before. For them to meet aunts and uncles they'd only heard about and to visit places that I used to visit when I was their age.

"I was coming to a free country. A free Slovakia had been a dream for the past one thousand years, and I just happened to be the one who lived in the era when it happened. I felt so lucky. I got to meet a lot of people who represented different generations of defectors. People who ran to save their lives. Many people who ran died and didn't get a chance to see a free Slovakia, and then you consider yourself lucky."

The ferry was about to board. Passengers who were standing outside enjoying the morning like us began climbing back in their cars and turning on their engines. I thanked Stastny for our conversation. Suddenly, I felt lucky too.

When we arrived on the mainland, the team went on to its Vancouver hotel. I got off the ferry so that I could return home for a few hours before the game.

"So," my wife said. "It all ends tonight."

"It all ends tonight."

A few messages from friends were waiting for me. It seemed that I would have some fans in the stands of the Pacific Coliseum for my last game. I tried to get some sleep that afternoon. I wanted to be particularly rested for my swan song so that I might find the additional energy to help me put a shot past the opposing goalie. But, try as I might, I had no luck sleeping. All I could think about was that my journey with the Oldtimers was just about over.

I thought about the laughs I had shared from Inuvik to Red Deer, from Fairbanks to Winnipeg. I thought about wonderful conversations too, and new friends, and a knowledge and understanding of the NHL that I never had before. I had started on this adventure with so many questions. I wondered, for instance, if the careers of today's NHL players could ever be as colourful and story-filled as the careers of the players from yesterday. I wondered, too, why people in the towns we visited on the tour still cared about these guys long after their careers had ended. And would they give today's players the same kind of warm reception if they came to town?

The answer to my first question could only be no. A lot has changed since Johnny Bower was a player and since Tiger Williams and Paul Reinhart played in the NHL. The game is more demanding. And as all the Oldtimers noted, there is far more money at stake today than before. As a result, today's players are less likely to take the kinds of chances that players did years ago. When players got into a bar fight twenty years ago, it was news for a day. Today, it's news for weeks and is rerun on "Sports Centre" six times a day. Who needed that headache? Ask Sergei Fedorov what it was like to get nabbed for driving under the influence in today's NHL.

Because there is so much more at stake today, because the competition for jobs is now so fierce, players would be crazy to stay out drinking until two or three or four in the morning. When half your teammates did it, and your coach too, it was no big deal—but that was twenty years ago.

All this is not to say that today's players will leave the game without stories of their own. You can't play in the NHL without gathering some stories, especially if you played for a coach like Mike Keenan. It's just that the stories won't likely be as juicy, or as jaw-dropping in the telling. But if you asked a player pulling down two, three, four million U.S. dollars a season what he'd rather have—more stories and less money or less stories and more money—you know what he'd take. The money. And who could blame him?

As for why people still cared about the Oldtimers years after the flame had gone out on their careers, well, that was easy. And I think Paul Reinhart said it best when he offered that the money today's NHL players made has completely changed the fan's perception of them. In the opinion of fans today, Tony Amonte or Jeremy Roenick or Mats Sundin don't play for the love of the game but for the love of the greenback. Rightly or wrongly, the perception exists that Tiger Williams and Marcel Dionne and Steve

Shutt—all of whom loved a dollar as much as the next guy—played the game before greed took over and ruined it forever.

Finally, the Oldtimers were a nostalgic treat for many. For those who showed up to watch them, watching Guy Lapointe and Darryl Sittler and Mark Napier brought them back to a cherished time in their lives, maybe a time when things were a little simpler. For some people, watching the Oldtimers connected them to memories of their parents, to a father who took a son to his first NHL game at Maple Leaf Gardens, the Montreal Forum, even the Coliseum in Edmonton, to watch the glorious Canadiens of the 1970s or the beautiful Oilers of the 1980s. Before the NHL game became slower and boring and not as much fun to watch.

I WAS WITH MY TEAMMATES for the last time, sitting in a dressing room at the Pacific Coliseum and wrapping tape around my hockey socks.

"We'll try and get you one tonight, buddy," said Mark Napier, who was sitting beside me.

"Hey, guys, let's try and get the rookie one tonight!" Napier screamed to the room. "He's retiring after the game."

"Let's try and build up a pretty good lead then, before we put him on the ice," someone else replied. Guffaws erupted around the room. A ball of sock tape flew by my ear.

I didn't score in my last game. But I did play with Darryl Sittler and Steve Shutt, and I was on the ice with Peter Stastny, too. I would feed a perfect pass to Mark Napier and miss a wide-open net. And when it was over, and when the crowd stood and cheered the Oldtimers, I raised my stick in the air just the way Wayne Gretzky did at Madison Square Garden in New York on the night he retired. Just for the fun of it.

Back in the dressing room, the guys didn't waste much time giving it to me.

"If you can't score on an open net, there's not much we can do to help you," said Moose Dupont.

"Yeah," another teammate yelled out. "Even Moose could have scored on that one."

"Ah, *tabernac,*" Moose shot back.

I took off my jersey and hung it up behind me. I loosened my skates and leaned back against the dressing room wall. Mark Napier walked over and handed me a cold one.

"Sorry we couldn't get you one, buddy," he said.

"Ah, no problem," I said. "I had my chances."

We clanked our beers together and each took a long sip. It felt good.

"It's been a good trip," Napier said.

I smiled back.

"It's been a great trip, Naps," I replied. "The trip of a lifetime."

EPILOGUE

Six weeks after the tour ended, Tiger Williams and I met for a beer in the same pub where we had enjoyed several rounds with Doug Gilmour of the Montreal Canadiens eight months earlier. The tour had yet to begin then, and Gilmour was lamenting his team's lousy start and talking about quitting the game once and for all.

Now here we were, sitting at the same table, watching Gilmour on television playing in the second round of the Stanley Cup playoffs.

"Pretty amazing, isn't it?" Tiger said, as we watched Gilmour skate onto the ice for the start of the game. "To think of where his head was when we talked to him and where it must be now. That's the beauty of this game."

I wanted to talk to Tiger a bit more about his career. About how it ended and what he missed most about it. I had explored this terrain with other players on the tour, such as Gary Nylund, but I knew Tiger would also have a different story from everyone else's. I knew that he was capable of exposing something else about the game, and the people who played it and ran it, that I hadn't thought about before. And I also knew that he was bound to have a story or two.

"Was it hard to give up hockey?" I asked Williams, as our beers arrived.

"I didn't give up hockey," he said. "Hockey gave up me."

And then Tiger began to tell the story of the day it all ended for him.

After nearly six seasons with the Toronto Maple Leafs, just over four with the Canucks, a few in Los Angeles and fifty-five mostly forgettable games with Detroit, Tiger had landed in Hartford at the beginning of the 1987–88 season. He'd been traded there by the L.A. Kings for cash.

With the Whalers, Williams played in 26 games, scoring 6 goals, adding zero assists and racking up 87 minutes in penalties. On March 11 of the new year, the day before the NHL trading deadline, Williams was at the Hartford airport with the rest of his team. They were scheduled to fly to Montreal for a game the next night. As it turned out, his wife, Brenda, and two young children at the time—Ben, who was ten, and Clancy, who was eight—were also at the airport waiting to leave on a plane.

"My dad was dying of cancer back in Weyburn," Tiger explained. "And it was spring break, so Brenda thought she'd take the kids and go visit Dad. So I'm just about to board the team flight, and I've got the kids' hands and I'm telling them that when they see grandpa he's not going to look the same or be the same because he's been real sick. Everyone's really emotional and the kids are teary-eyed and all that, but anyway as I'm just about to board the plane one of the Hartford management guys comes up to me and says: 'Oh, Tiger, we forgot to tell you. We released you earlier today.'"

Williams was stunned. So were his kids and wife, who quickly determined what it meant.

"All of a sudden I've got three people crying pretty hard," Williams recalled. "And it was no big deal, except that my wife and kids were right there, right there, when the guy told me. It would have been nice if it had been done in a more appropriate manner, but because it was Emile Francis who was GM at the time and the Hartford Whalers, they knew no other way. They had no class. Never did have any class. Never would have any class. So there I was, with no job and my wife and two kids crying their eyes out."

The other thing Williams didn't have was an agent. Since his first year in the league Williams did all his negotiating himself, thereby avoiding having to give some of his hard-earned cash to someone else. But what it meant now was that he didn't happen to have the home phone numbers of every GM in the league to see if someone might be interested in his services for the remainder of the season.

He talked to Glen Sather in Edmonton, who did show interest, but not at the salary Williams was making. As it turned out, Williams still had two years left on the contract that he had signed with L.A. and that Hartford had assumed in the trade. If he did nothing for the next two seasons, he would still get paid.

That's precisely what would happen.

"I thought, to hell with that," said Williams, recalling why he did not agree to a pay cut to continue playing with another team. "I had spent my whole career helping other people. Now it was time to help myself. So that's the way it ended, and, you know, thousands of guys have their careers end just the same way."

ASK MOST NHL HOCKEY PLAYERS what they miss most about the game when they retire, and they'll say the camaraderie. The jokes in the dressing room. The drinks on the road. The stories. The hundreds and hundreds of stories. And Williams missed all that when he was no longer playing the game, to be sure. But what he missed even more was the chase.

"I loved the process," Williams said, as we watched the Carolina Hurricanes take an early 1–0 lead over the Canadiens. "The great thing about hockey is you get instant reward and instant failure. You don't have to wait for the quarterly financial statements to come out to see how you've been doing. When the game's over, it's there. You either won it or you lost it, and after a week you've either lost four in a row or won three and tied one, and I like that.

"But you know, I missed stupid little things too. Like the fact that I roomed with some guy who got four shifts a game and took a shot off the ankle and it swelled up the size of a football, and there he is sleeping with his foot in a pail of water and I'm waking up every twenty minutes to make sure he's okay, and the next night we're playing together. You know, you'll never, ever have that feeling doing anything else."

Up on the television screen, the Hurricanes have scored again. Gilmour, however, was playing his usual tenacious game. Skating like someone years younger, competing like someone fighting for his NHL job instead of someone nearing the end of his nineteenth season.

"When we were here eight months ago or whenever it was, he was so disappointed and was thinking of packing it in," Tiger said as we watched the game. "What did we say to him that night? We said, 'Don't quit. We want you to keep going.' I bet he's glad he did now."

We stayed a little longer. Ordered a couple more rounds and talked about whether there would be an Oldtimers tour in ten years time. Tiger didn't think so. It would probably be viewed as too much work for too little return for the modern player, who would make millions more than players of Tiger's generation. Who needed to tour around economy-class, staying in three-star hotels? But the Oldtimers tour wasn't about money, I said, it was still about the one thing players loved the most about hockey.

The game. And the stories that surrounded it.

"You know what Gary Nylund said was the reason he regretted not trying to get a few more seasons out of his bad knee?" I said to Tiger.

"No, what?"

"He said he would have had three more years of stories," I replied. "And I think that's what the Oldtimers tour is mostly about anyway. Stories. Guys telling stories. Trying to top one another. Making something fairly mundane sound absolutely hilarious in the retelling. That's why no one ever shuts up. Everyone has a million stories."

"Yes," Tiger laughed. "There are some great stories."

Up on the screen, our one-time drinking buddy had just received a penalty. He skated to the box wearing a Doug Gilmour scowl, slamming the door in disgust behind him. In a split-second there was glass everywhere.

"Look at that!" Tiger howled. "Gilmour smashed the window in the penalty box. Hey, that should be how you end the book."

It sounded like a good idea to me.